MIND

CONTROL

IN THE

UNITED
STATES

BY STEVEN JACOBSON

INTRODUCTION BY ANTONY C. SUTTON

REVISED AND UPDATED EDITION

2015 Revised and Updated Edition
Dauphin Publications Inc.
www.daupub.com
ISBN: 978-1-939438-16-4

INVOCATION

"O Master of the Great White Lodge,

Lord of all the religions of the world,

Come down again to the earth that needs Thee,

And help the nations that are longing for Thy presence.

Speak the word of peace

Which shall make the peoples to cease from their quarrellings.

Speak the word of brotherhood

Which shall make the warring classes and castes to know themselves as one.

Come in the might of Thy Love,

Come in the splendor of Thy Power,

And save the world which is longing for Thy Coming,

O Thou who are the Teacher alike of angels and of men." *

The exact contrary of what is generally believed is often the truth.

- Jean de La Bruyére (1645-1696)

*From the edition of "The Gospel of the Holy Twelve" published by Edson (Printers) Limited, London in 1923.

i

ABOUT THE AUTHOR

Steven Jacobson has been investigating the mind control issue for more than three decades. He is a graduate of the Boston University School of Communications and worked in the film industry for 13 years. As an editor he saw how simple it is to change the meaning of an event or of what someone says through editing. But he did not fully appreciate the extent to which we are all manipulated and controlled by mass media (even those who work in it) until he was given the results of private research investigating mental programming, deprogramming and reprogramming. His father was a hypnotist, researcher and consultant to the medical profession for more than 20 years. He turned over his research to Steven in 1980, which led him to leave the career he was pursuing to research mind control, discovering that mind control is being used on an unsuspecting public. The book *Mind Control in the United States*, published in 1985, was the result, followed by the audio presentation *Mind Control in America* in 1991 and *Wake-Up America* in 1995. He was interviewed on numerous radio talk shows for about a dozen years, when he stopped to focus on his spiritual practice and study. *Mind Control in the United States* has now been revised and updated in this 2015 edition for the benefit of all the people who are influenced by this issue.

For more information, visit Steven Jacobson's website:
www.mindcontrolinamerica.com

TABLE OF CONTENTS

PREFACE TO THE REVISED EDITION

We live in a controlled environment, a "virtual reality," where few people realize the extent to which we are manipulated and controlled by unseen forces. Present day society is the most manipulated and controlled society in history as a result of the programming and conditioning we all undergo through mass media and public education. Much of what we "know" as a society is indoctrinated into us at an early age. Most people do not give much thought to why they believe some of the things that they do. Things are accepted as true that may not be simply as the result of habit. Many of the things that people believe are never questioned, especially when the information has come from a trusted source. People can be led to believe something that is not true when the information is carefully timed, presented by an accepted and respected authority and repeated over and over again until acceptance of its truth and accuracy becomes a conditioned response. Thus there is the tendency to accept the information as true without thinking about it whenever it is presented again.

The mind automatically and involuntarily rejects information that is not consistent with what we already believe. There is a term for this. It is called "cognitive dissonance." It means that it is difficult for some people and nearly impossible for others to consider information that does not fit into their preconditioned mind-set, even if that information is exactly what they need to consider. We do not see things as they are, but rather "as we are." In order to receive the most benefit from the information presented, it is requested that you keep an open mind as you begin this guided tour into the world of mind control.

Mind Control in the United States was originally published in 1985 as an overview of the topic and placing it in a spiritual context. The mind control issue is first and foremost a spiritual issue because the mind is the gateway to the soul. And spiritual consciousness is the only solution to the problems and suffering of material existence. This revised edition contains most of the content of the original with some revisions, clarifications, updates, commentary and new material. It is hoped that this will be helpful to the reader in looking at the world and current events from a new perspective, "outside the box" of conventional consensus "reality." The circumstances, conditions and events seen in the outer world are a reflection of the inner collective consciousness of mankind under the influence of unseen forces. The problems of life are no different today than they were 2,000 years ago. The solution is also the same. To help break the spell of mind control and empower the public to fend off the relentless assault on their mental, psychological, emotional and spiritual integrity is the purpose of this little book in length with a big message inside for your consideration.

Steven Jacobson

North Carolina, 2015

MIND CONTROL IS BEING USED ON AN UNSUSPECTING PUBLIC. MIND CONTROL IS BEING USED ON AN UNSUSPECTING PUBLIC.
MIND CONTROL IS BEING USED ON AN UNSUSPECTING PUBLIC. MIND CONTROL IS BEING USED ON AN UNSUSPECTING PUBLIC.
MIND CONTROL IS BEING USED ON AN UNSUSPECTING PUBLIC. MIND CONTROL IS BEING USED ON AN UNSUSPECTING PUBLIC.
MIND CONTROL IS BEING USED ON AN UNSUSPECTING PUBLIC. MIND CONTROL IS BEING USED ON AN UNSUSPECTING PUBLIC.
MIND CONTROL IS BEING USED ON AN UNSUSPECTING PUBLIC. MIND CONTROL IS BEING USED ON AN UNSUSPECTING PUBLIC.

SECTION 1
Introduction

MIND CONTROL IS BEING USED ON AN UNSUSPECTING PUBLIC. MIND CONTROL IS BEING USED ON AN UNSUSPECTING PUBLIC.
MIND CONTROL IS BEING USED ON AN UNSUSPECTING PUBLIC. MIND CONTROL IS BEING USED ON AN UNSUSPECTING PUBLIC.
MIND CONTROL IS BEING USED ON AN UNSUSPECTING PUBLIC. MIND CONTROL IS BEING USED ON AN UNSUSPECTING PUBLIC.
MIND CONTROL IS BEING USED ON AN UNSUSPECTING PUBLIC. MIND CONTROL IS BEING USED ON AN UNSUSPECTING PUBLIC.
MIND CONTROL IS BEING USED ON AN UNSUSPECTING PUBLIC. MIND CONTROL IS BEING USED ON AN UNSUSPECTING PUBLIC.
MIND CONTROL IS BEING USED ON AN UNSUSPECTING PUBLIC. MIND CONTROL IS BEING USED ON AN UNSUSPECTING PUBLIC.
MIND CONTROL IS BEING USED ON AN UNSUSPECTING PUBLIC. MIND CONTROL IS BEING USED ON AN UNSUSPECTING PUBLIC.
MIND CONTROL IS BEING USED ON AN UNSUSPECTING PUBLIC. MIND CONTROL IS BEING USED ON AN UNSUSPECTING PUBLIC.
MIND CONTROL IS BEING USED ON AN UNSUSPECTING PUBLIC. MIND CONTROL IS BEING USED ON AN UNSUSPECTING PUBLIC.
MIND CONTROL IS BEING USED ON AN UNSUSPECTING PUBLIC. MIND CONTROL IS BEING USED ON AN UNSUSPECTING PUBLIC.

The most effective way to protect yourself from subconscious manipulation is to be aware of how it works.

Steven Jacobson, author of *Mind Control in the United States*, is a film technician experienced in subliminal techniques used in the communication media.

Subliminal perception is a process, a deliberate process created by communications technicians, by which you receive and respond to information and instructions without being *consciously* aware of the instructions.

Scary? You bet your life it is. And as Jacobson details in this book it is happening in America today.

Mind Control in the United States is an introduction to the history and practice of subliminal communication. It outlines the principles of mental programming, i.e., that an initial distraction must be followed by repetitive commands, and it tells you how these ideas are implemented.

Further, the book tells you when and where it has been used. Jacobson's examples range from In-Flight Motion Pictures, Inc. and its on-board films to general audience movies such as *Reefer Madness, The Exorcist, and My World Dies Screaming*. The effects on audiences are graphically described.

The case of the movie *The Exorcist* is especially interesting. William Peter Blatty, author of the book and producer of the movie, is a former CIA operative. Blatty had an extensive career in government psychological manipulations. One has to be pretty naive to argue there is no connection between Blatty's CIA career and his choice of communications techniques.

Similarly, subliminal techniques have been used on radio and television. Current research has moved heavily into extra sensory perception (ESP), the use of meditation, and marijuana to generate altered states of consciousness. Out-of-body experiences are apparently better documented as research has progressed far beyond general belief.

Just who is responsible for this intrusive experimentation with free individuals in a free society?

Author Jacobson presents example after example identifying the so-called Eastern Establishment, that coterie made up of the Council on Foreign Relations, the Bilderbergers, and other assorted elitists as the primary source. Even at the White House level, deception was practiced not only by that master deceiver, Richard Nixon, but also by Presidents Johnson, Carter, and Reagan. At the corporate level every large advertising agency has experimented with subliminal manipulation.

Finally, deception has been used to disguise the pervasive erosion of our constitutionally guaranteed freedoms.

Unfortunately for us, George Orwell's *1984* was right on schedule. What is alarming is that very, very few citizens realize that deception is already part of the social framework. We don't know that 1984 has already arrived because we have been conditioned not to know.

By the same means, the media has created a state of inner turmoil in citizens through portrayal of violence and chaos and irrational behavior. This inner state is reflected in the chaotic world outside.

What can you do? Hopefully this book will increase your sense of skepticism when it comes to the establishment and its representatives. Less obviously, you do have a duty to freedom to find the truth and spread the truth.

Mind Control in the United States will be invaluable in this task. At least you will know who tried to brainwash you and how they tried.

ANTONY C. SUTTON
California, 1985

MIND CONTROL IS BEING USED ON AN UNSUSPECTING PUBLIC. MIND CONTROL IS BEING USED ON AN UNSUSPECTING PUBLIC.
MIND CONTROL IS BEING USED ON AN UNSUSPECTING PUBLIC. MIND CONTROL IS BEING USED ON AN UNSUSPECTING PUBLIC.
MIND CONTROL IS BEING USED ON AN UNSUSPECTING PUBLIC. MIND CONTROL IS BEING USED ON AN UNSUSPECTING PUBLIC.
MIND CONTROL IS BEING USED ON AN UNSUSPECTING PUBLIC. MIND CONTROL IS BEING USED ON AN UNSUSPECTING PUBLIC.
MIND CONTROL IS BEING USED ON AN UNSUSPECTING PUBLIC. MIND CONTROL IS BEING USED ON AN UNSUSPECTING PUBLIC.
MIND CONTROL IS BEING USED ON AN UNSUSPECTING PUBLIC. MIND CONTROL IS BEING USED ON AN UNSUSPECTING PUBLIC.

SECTION 2
NINETEEN EIGHTY-FOUR

MIND CONTROL IS BEING USED ON AN UNSUSPECTING PUBLIC. MIND CONTROL IS BEING USED ON AN UNSUSPECTING PUBLIC.
MIND CONTROL IS BEING USED ON AN UNSUSPECTING PUBLIC. MIND CONTROL IS BEING USED ON AN UNSUSPECTING PUBLIC.
MIND CONTROL IS BEING USED ON AN UNSUSPECTING PUBLIC. MIND CONTROL IS BEING USED ON AN UNSUSPECTING PUBLIC.
MIND CONTROL IS BEING USED ON AN UNSUSPECTING PUBLIC. MIND CONTROL IS BEING USED ON AN UNSUSPECTING PUBLIC.
MIND CONTROL IS BEING USED ON AN UNSUSPECTING PUBLIC. MIND CONTROL IS BEING USED ON AN UNSUSPECTING PUBLIC.
MIND CONTROL IS BEING USED ON AN UNSUSPECTING PUBLIC. MIND CONTROL IS BEING USED ON AN UNSUSPECTING PUBLIC.
MIND CONTROL IS BEING USED ON AN UNSUSPECTING PUBLIC. MIND CONTROL IS BEING USED ON AN UNSUSPECTING PUBLIC.

In the book *1984*, George Orwell warns that people are in danger of losing their human qualities and freedom of mind without being aware of it while it is happening because of psychological engineering. We have learned to expect the Soviet Union and the People's Republic of China to use "mind control" on its citizens, but not the "free world." Nevertheless, the same techniques are being used in the United States. The most effective way to protect yourself from subconscious manipulation is by being aware of how it works. The techniques used to enslave the mind are the same used to free it.

COMMENTARY: The use of social engineering to influence and control what people think makes a mockery of the informed consent of the governed – the very cornerstone of the Constitution. The programming and conditioning of the mind is not a legitimate function of government. The ultimate control is to control people without their conscious awareness. It is the hallmark of tyranny.

MIND CONTROL IS BEING USED ON AN UNSUSPECTING PUBLIC. MIND CONTROL IS BEING USED ON AN UNSUSPECTING PUBLIC.
MIND CONTROL IS BEING USED ON AN UNSUSPECTING PUBLIC. MIND CONTROL IS BEING USED ON AN UNSUSPECTING PUBLIC.
MIND CONTROL IS BEING USED ON AN UNSUS   IS BEING USED ON AN UNSUSPECTING PUBLIC.
MIND CONTROL IS BEING USED ON AN UNS   IS BEING USED ON AN UNSUSPECTING PUBLIC.
MIND CONTROL IS BEING USED ON AN UNS   IS BEING USED ON AN UNSUSPECTING PUBLIC.
MIND CONTROL IS BEING USED ON AN UNS   IS BEING USED ON AN UNSUSPECTING PUBLIC.
MIND CONTROL IS BEING USED ON AN UNSUSPECTING PUBLIC.   IS BEING USED ON AN UNSUSPECTING PUBLIC.
MIND CONTROL IS BEING USED ON AN   ING PUBLIC.   ING USED ON AN UNSUSPECTING PUBLIC.
MIND CONTROL IS BEING USED ON AN   ING USED ON AN UNSUSPECTING PUBLIC.
MIND CONTROL IS BEING USED ON AN   ING USED ON AN UNSUSPECTING PUBLIC.
MIND CONTROL IS BEING USED ON AN UNSUSPECTING PUBLIC.   ING USED ON AN UNSUSPECTING PUBLIC.
MIND CONTROL IS BEING USED ON AN UNSUSPECTING PUBLIC. MIND CONTROL IS BEING USED ON AN UNSUSPECTING PUBLIC.
MIND CONTROL IS BE   UNSUSPECTING PUBLIC.
MIND CONTROL IS BE   UNSUSPECTING PUBLIC.
MIND CONTROL IS BE   UNSUSPECTING PUBLIC.
MIND CONTROL IS BEING USED ON AN UNSUSPECTING PUBLIC. MIND CONTROL IS BEING USED ON AN UNSUSPECTING PUBLIC.
MIND CONTROL IS BEING USED ON AN UNSUSPECTING PUBLIC. MIND CONTROL IS BEING USED ON AN UNSUSPECTING PUBLIC.
MIND CONTROL IS BEING USED ON AN UNSUSPECTING PUBLIC. MIND CONTROL IS BEING USED ON AN UNSUSPECTING PUBLIC.
MIND CONTROL IS BEING USED ON AN UNSUSPECTING PUBLIC. MIND CONTROL IS BEING USED ON AN UNSUSPECTING PUBLIC.

SECTION 3
Principles of
Mental Programming

The most effective way to conquer a man is to capture his mind. Control a man's mind and you control his body. Most people don't pay conscious attention to the things that affect them subconsciously. They don't usually know what to look for. However, when pointed to, these things can be recognized and understood.

The principles of mind control, hypnotic suggestion and, mental programming are ancient (the term used doesn't matter, the principles remain the same). **The goal is to suspend the thought processes of the conscious mind** to cause a state of mind that is just like "day dreaming." Stop conscious thought and the mind is in its most suggestible state and is more receptive to programming than at any other time. Therefore, **the first principle of mind control is distraction**. Distraction focuses the attention of the conscious mind on one or more of the five senses (sight, sound, touch, smell and taste) in order to program the subconscious mind.

All men do not think the same thoughts, but all men think with the same mechanism–the brain. One part of the brain works things out one step at a time just like a computer. This is the language-using left side of the brain which is also identified as the conscious mind. The tools of the conscious mind are words (spoken, written and thought) and pictures and sounds. The conscious mind discriminates, evaluates, accepts or rejects. Sometimes the more you think about a problem, the further you get from finding a solution to it. When this happens, you make decisions based on how you feel. "I didn't arrive at my understanding of the fundamental laws of the universe through my rational mind," said Albert Einstein.[1] The powers of intuition are the

4

powers of the subconscious mind. The right side of the brain is the center of intuition, creativity, emotion.[2]

"Use The Force, Luke. The Force is an energy field created by all living things. Trust your feelings, not the computer." The Force in *Star Wars* is Hollywood's version of an ancient principle. Think of your subconscious mind as your link with "The Force." Also think of your subconscious mind as your own personal energy source. Now imagine your conscious thoughts directing this energy source and drawing power from "The Force." This is the relationship of the conscious mind to the subconscious. **What the conscious mind believes, the subconscious acts on**. It works like programming a computer. You feed information into a computer, and the computer acts on it. However, if the information you feed into the computer is wrong, it still acts on it! If you give yourself incorrect information or if others give you incorrect information, the memory banks of your subconscious mind do not correct the error but act on it!

When you stop conscious thinking and let your mind go blank, then your mind is in its most suggestible state. It is in this state of mind where you are the most receptive to mental programming. This state of mind is just like "day dreaming." Now remember the first principle behind mental programming. That principle is distraction. **Distraction focuses the attention of the conscious mind on one or more of the five senses in order to program the subconscious mind**. The same principle applies to all illusion, magic and propaganda.

The second principle of mental programming is repetition. Distraction and repetition represent the learning process. Picture yourself studying in school. You are reading a book. Your eyes are focused on the page of the book. The words on the page are the conscious distraction for your eyes. The information you are reading is being programmed directly to your subconscious mind. You are not consciously analyzing the material you are reading until you look away from the page and think about it. It is at this point you have the opportunity to analyze the information you have just read and accept it as true or reject it as false. If you accept the information as true, it is programmed that way to your subconscious mind. If you reject the information as false, that is programmed to your subconscious mind. However, if you don't know if the information is true or not, a curious thing happens. Your trust in the source of the information determines whether or not you accept the information. If you do not believe that a book could contain information that was false (unintentionally or intentionally), then you would accept its information as true even if you weren't sure or didn't understand it. This is especially true in school where there is pressure to accept what is presented as true because that is what is expected and that determines your grade and your future. **Repetition of the information imbeds it in your subconscious mind so that your acceptance of its truth (accuracy) becomes a conditioned response. You accept this information as true without thinking whenever it is presented to you again.**

COMMENTARY: The dictionary defines the word "mind" as the place where thinking occurs. The word "control" means to regulate, direct or exercise control over. The term "mind control" refers to a broad spectrum of psychological techniques, both internal and external, ranging from simple control of information to trauma-based mind control (torture), electro-magnetic mind control (implantation of thoughts and feelings by radio frequency transmission) and surgical implants designed to regulate, direct and exercise control over the mind and thus over thinking, feeling, willing, behavior and memory.

SECTION 4

The Power of Music

Think back to a time when you have been saddened by a song. It may have brought a tear. You might have felt it in your stomach as a change in muscle tension. The power of music has been recognized throughout history. Plato and Aristotle believed that people could be controlled by music. It affects your body, your mind and your emotions. Sound causes changes in your body chemistry, blood pressure, breathing and digestion. Even sound that you cannot hear affects you. Low frequency "infrasonic" sounds affect your internal organs and can cause headaches, nausea, dizziness and fatigue. Fast music will speed up the nervous system while slow music will slow it down. Your entire body is sensitive to sound. Sounds vibrate in different parts of the body. Low tones will vibrate in the lower parts of your body, and high tones will vibrate in the higher portions and on into the head.[3]

Sixties rock superstar Jimi Hendrix said: **"You can hypnotize people with music, and when you get them at their weakest point you can preach into their subconscious whatever you want to say."**[4] Much of today's popular rock music is built around a heavy bass pattern louder than the melody. These loud, low frequency vibrations and the driving beat of most rock music affect the pituitary gland. The pituitary gland produces hormones that control the sexual responses of males and females.[5] These low frequency vibrations vibrate in the lower parts of your body so that the music "feels" good.

It is important to note that the lyrics of many rock songs are not clearly distinguishable consciously. Now remember your subconscious mind hears all. Repetition of the message is mental programming. Research indicates that repeated hearings, whether sought out or not, yield acceptance and even liking.[6] When you do not hear the message clearly, you cannot make the conscious choice to accept or reject it. When you cannot make that choice or when that choice is taken away from you, the message is programmed directly to your subconscious mind without your knowing it, thus circumventing analysis and choice in accepting the content of the message. In time the effects of this kind of programming will appear. These effects can be physical, psychological and emotional. *Most people don't pay conscious attention to the things that affect them subconsciously because they don't know what to look for. However, when pointed to, these things are recognized and understood.*

It has been well-established by research that the subconscious mind is capable of reading mirror images, even upside-down mirror images.[7] This also applies to words spoken or sung backwards. This phenomenon is called backward masking.[8] The Beatles started using backward masking on their *White Album* with the song *Revolution Number Nine*. The song repeatedly says, "number nine, number nine." Played backwards it becomes "turn me on, dead man."[9] Rumors swept the world, "Paul is Dead!" Material on Paul's death was embedded in the *Magical Mystery Tour* album in the last few grooves of the song *Strawberry Fields*. A low volume voice says, "I buried Paul."[10]

About twenty-four hundred years ago, Plato demanded strict censorship over popular music in his utopian *Republic*.[11] In Nazi Germany, the government used music to create a state of mind in the German people.[12] In the Soviet Union, a state commission determined the kind of music to be heard. If music was such a powerful tool for control in the Soviet Union, it can be used in the same way in the United States and the rest of the world. Ayotollah Khomeini, leader of Iran, placed tight controls on music broadcasting and banned certain types of music as a threat to his rule.[13] In Orwell's *1984*, music is tightly controlled because of its power to communicate and influence human behavior.

COMMENTARY: Confucius said: *"If one should desire to know whether a kingdom is well-governed, if its morals are good or bad, the quality of its music will furnish the answer."*

Change in musical style is inevitably followed by a change in politics and morality. Change swept western civilization, not just the United States, in the 1960's that was brought about by a change in popular music by the British invasion of The Beatles, the Rolling Stones and other rock groups. More recently, rap and hip-hop music has impacted culture across all ethnic and socio-economic demographics among young people around the world. Many ancient civilizations recognized that music plays an important role in determining the character and direction of society. They believed that music possesses a tangible power than can be used to bring about change within an individual and society. Such power in the hands of evil and ignorant men would have dire consequences for society.

The most successful propaganda uses the arts as a delivery system. Art is a way of seeing and what we see in art defines what we understand to be "reality". Reality is a state of mind. Change your state of mind and you change reality. The population has been conditioned by a mass media created reality. Long-term exposure to this *artificial reality* cannot help but have an enormous impact on the social, political and spiritual life of the nation. Many people, especially young people, accept unquestioningly the reality presented by the media. Popular culture (movies, television and music) carries messages about how society works, what's right and wrong and how people should behave. Entertainment is not value-free. It has ideological content and presents a world view that influences those who watch the programming. Entertainment is not just entertainment. It is also propaganda.

MIND CONTROL IS BEING USED ON AN UNSUSPECTING PUBLIC. MIND CONTROL IS BEING USED ON AN UNSUSPECTING PUBLIC.
MIND CONTROL IS BEING USED ON AN UNSUSPECTING PUBLIC. MIND CONTROL IS BEING USED ON AN UNSUSPECTING PUBLIC.
MIND CONTROL IS BEING USED ON AN UNSUSPECTING PUBLIC. MIND CONTROL IS BEING USED ON AN UNSUSPECTING PUBLIC.
MIND CONTROL IS BEING USED ON AN UNSUSPECTING PUBLIC. MIND CONTROL IS BEING USED ON AN UNSUSPECTING PUBLIC.
MIND CONTROL IS BEING USED ON AN UNSUSPECTING PUBLIC. MIND CONTROL IS BEING USED ON AN UNSUSPECTING PUBLIC.
MIND CONTROL IS BEING USED ON AN UNS   S BEING USED ON AN UNSUSPECTING PUBLIC.
MIND CONTROL IS BEING USED ON AN UNS   BEING USED ON AN UNSUSPECTING PUBLIC.
MIND CONTROL IS BEING USED ON AN UNS   BEING USED ON AN UNSUSPECTING PUBLIC.
MIND CONTROL IS BEING USED ON AN UNSUSPECTING PUBLIC. MIND CONTROL IS BEING USED ON AN UNSUSPECTING PUBLIC.
MIND CONTROL IS BEING USED ON AN UNSUSPECTING PUBLIC. MIND CONTROL IS BEING USED ON AN UNSUSPECTING PUBLIC.
MIND CONTROL IS BEING USED ON AN UNSUSPECTING PUBLIC. MIND CONTROL IS BEING USED ON AN UNSUSPECTING PUBLIC.
MIND CONTROL IS BEING USED ON AN UNSUSPECTING PUBLIC. MIND CONTROL IS BEING USED ON AN UNSUSPECTING PUBLIC.
MIND CONTROL IS BEING USED ON AN UNSUSPECTING PUBLIC. MIND CONTROL IS BEING USED ON AN UNSUSPECTING PUBLIC.
MIND CONTROL IS BEING USED ON AN UNSUSPECTING PUBLIC. MIND CONTROL IS BEING USED ON AN UNSUSPECTING PUBLIC.
MIND CONTROL IS BEING USED ON AN UNSUSPECTING PUBLIC. MIND CONTROL IS BEING USED ON AN UNSUSPECTING PUBLIC.
MIND CONTROL IS BEING USED ON AN UNSUSPECTING PUBLIC. MIND CONTROL IS BEING USED ON AN UNSUSPECTING PUBLIC.
MIND CONTROL IS BEING USED ON AN UNSUSPECTING PUBLIC. MIND CONTROL IS BEING USED ON AN UNSUSPECTING PUBLIC.
MIND CONTROL IS BEING USED ON AN UNSUSPECTING PUBLIC. MIND CONTROL IS BEING USED ON AN UNSUSPECTING PUBLIC.
MIND CONTROL IS BEING USED ON AN UNSUSPECTING PUBLIC. MIND CONTROL IS BEING USED ON AN UNSUSPECTING PUBLIC.

SECTION 5

TV, Radio and Movies

Watching television often creates an altered state of consciousness, because the television screen, while appearing static, actually flickers. What causes you to go into an altered state? In hypnosis, it is actually body relaxation and a carefully patterned voice roll. The hypnotist speaks with a regular beat, as if matching his words to a metronome.[14] **In fact, any repeating light or sound pattern can lead you into the hypnotic state of mind**—a state of mind that is just like "day dreaming." This is an altered state of consciousness. Think of the times you have caught yourself staring blankly at the television screen, losing all sense of time and place. When you stop conscious thinking and your mind goes blank, then your mind is in its most suggestible state. It is in this state of mind where you are the most receptive to mental programming. Think of the many times you have seen flashing words in both local and national TV commercials. The flashing words are the conscious distraction for the eyes. While the eyes are being occupied, the message being spoken is programmed directly to your subconscious mind. Anything consciously perceived can be evaluated, criticized, discussed, argued, and possibly rejected. Any information programmed subliminally to your subconscious mind meets no resistance. This subliminal information is stored in your brain with an identification that will trigger a delayed alarm clock-reaction capable of influencing your behavior.[15]

On June 22, 1956, the British Broadcasting Corporation experimented with projecting subliminal images on television. Pictures were flashed on the screen too quickly to be seen consciously, but they did make an impression on the subconscious.[16] Subliminal perception is the process whereby you receive and respond to visual and sound information without being aware of it.[17] The message, in the form of printed words, pictures or voices, is presented either so rapidly or so faintly that you are not consciously aware of having seen or heard anything.[18] The BBC experiment was followed by an experiment by the Canadian Broadcasting Corporation doing the same thing: projecting subliminal images.[19] Mexico's *Televisa* commercial TV and radio network has experimented extensively with subliminal broadcast techniques.[20] In the U.S., TV station WTWO in Bangor, Maine conducted an experiment in November, 1957.[21]

Experiments were not limited to television. In 1958, radio station WAAF in Chicago broadcast "sub audible" commercials. Seattle's KOL broadcast hardly audible taped messages "below" the music played by its disc jockeys. "How about a cup of coffee?" was one, and "Someone's at the door" was another. Marketing researcher and psychologist James Vicary tested subliminal ads in a New Jersey movie theatre. "Hungry? Eat Popcorn" and "Drink Coca-Cola" were flashed on the screen at 1/3000 of a second every five seconds during the movie. Sales increased for popcorn and Coca-Cola.[22] On December 8, 1972, *The New York Times* reported that In-Flight Motion Pictures, Inc. would begin selling subliminal commercials embedded in the movies they would distribute to all the major airlines.[23] Stores across the country are reducing theft an average 30 to 50 percent by broadcasting subliminal messages such as "I will not steal."[24] Stimutech, Inc. of East Lansing, Michigan markets a computer video system that flashes subliminal messages on your television while you watch the regular programming. The subliminal messages are prepared by a team of psychologists to change the thinking patterns and behavior of the viewer.[25]

Using what was called the Precon Process, the picture of a skull and the word BLOOD were flashed subliminally on the screen in the movie *My World Dies Screaming*. Some words and images trigger strong emotional responses in people. Laboratory experiments show that people will react to words like BLOOD and to pictures of skulls with quickened pulse, faster breathing, sweating palms and other indications of heightened emotions.[26] *The Exorcist* used both subliminal sounds and pictures. A number of times during the movie, the face of Father Karras became a two-frame, full-screen death mask. Twenty-four frames of motion picture film are projected per second. The death mask flashed on the screen at 1/48 of a second.[27] The consciously unnoticed word PIG appears many time throughout the movie.[28]

The terrified squealing of pigs being slaughtered was mixed subtly into the sound track.[29] The buzzing sound of angry, agitated bees wove in and out of scenes throughout the film.[30] People really did faint in large numbers, many more became nauseous in varying degrees, a great many more had disturbing nightmares.[31] It is interesting to note that William Peter Blatty, the author of the novel and producer of the movie, is a former CIA operative who served as the policy-branch chief of the Psychological Warfare Division of the U.S. Air Force.[32] According to previously classified documents, the CIA tested subliminal manipulation in movie theatres during the late 1950s.[33]

The Bruce Lee "Kung-Fu" movie *Game of Death* illustrates how easy it is to manipulate what the audience thinks. Bruce Lee is billed as the star, but an actor impersonates him throughout the movie. Selective camera angles attempt to hide this. Close-ups of Lee from other movies are used to give the impression that Lee himself appears throughout the story. The difference in the background of these close-ups and changes in color give away the technique. This movie was put together with skillful editing to lead up to the climactic fight sequences that were shot with Bruce Lee.

"The foundation of film art is editing," wrote Russian film director Pudovkin in the preface of the German edition of his book on film techniques. In an experiment at the Moscow Film School, Lev Kuleshov created the impression of a single actress by joining the face of one woman, the torso of another, the hands of another, the legs of yet another. An anonymous British film technician is quoted in a front-page article in the *London Tribune*, August 5, 1949 saying: "We claim that with judicious cutting and an adroit use of camera angles, it is simple to make a fool of anybody. We can distort the emphasis and meaning of Ministers' speeches not only by cutting out statements but by simple use of long shot, medium shot, and close-up. For any statement said in close-up is given greater significance on the screen than one said in long shot. There is no end to the tricks we can play with this simple device."[34]

Some of the most spectacular footage of the San Francisco earthquake and fire in 1906 was faked. Newsreel companies often staged events. During the Mexican Revolution in 1914, they made arrangements with Pancho Villa to fight his battles in daylight and to wait until the cameras were in place before launching his attack. Much of the newsreel coverage of World War I was faked. *Literary Digest* printed an expose in its

November 13, 1915 issue. The practice of faking scenes of celebrities by employing impersonators was frequently used by *The March of Time* screen magazine. Known instances of content manufacture, re-creation, personality impersonation are documented by Raymond Fielding in *The American Newsreel.*

On October 30, 1938 the planet earth was invaded by men from Mars. . . not really, but many people thought so.

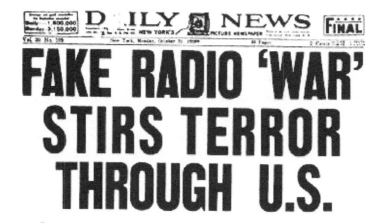

THE NEW YORK TIMES, Monday, October 31, 1938:

"A wave of mass hysteria seized thousands of radio listeners throughout the nation between 8:15 and 9:30 o'clock last night when a broadcast of a dramatization of H. G. Wells' fantasy, *The War of the Worlds,* led thousands to believe that an interplanetary conflict had started with invading Martians spreading wide death and destruction in New Jersey and New York."

"... we are ready to believe almost anything if it comes from a recognized authority," writes Howard Koch in his book *The Panic Broadcast.* Koch wrote the radio script performed by Orson Welles and his Mercury Theatre on CBS. Thousands fled from a crisis that had no existence except in their imaginations.

COMMENTARY: The dramatization of H.G. Wells' *War of the Worlds* was presented as a news broadcast with a cast of characters that included the anchorperson(s), correspondents reporting from the field and outside "experts" brought in to comment on new developments. Despite disclaimers, people thought they were listening to an authentic news broadcast. The public had already been programmed to accept the news broadcast format as the means for transmitting and receiving true, factual information. Produced on video tape for realism, the 1983 made-for-TV-movie *Special Bulletin* about terrorists exploding an atomic bomb in Charleston, South Carolina looks and sounds like a real news broadcast in every detail. Despite disclaimers, people thought they were watching an authentic news broadcast because they had already been programmed to accept the information presented in the news broadcast format.

Story-telling is the oldest means of transmitting information about how society works and what's right and wrong. There is not much difference between primitive man sitting fixated in front of the flickering light of a camp fire listening to stories about how society works and what's right and wrong from modern man sitting fixated in front of the flickering light of a television screen receiving information about how society works and what's right and wrong. Television is by far the most powerful weapon of psychological warfare in history.

Think for a moment about the way newscasters speak. The patterned speech of a newscaster is similar to that of a hypnotist. Local and national news anchors look directly into the camera and into the eyes of the viewing public. The eye contact made with the viewer is also a hypnotic technique. And a newscaster is also an accepted and respected authority figure, thus encouraging acceptance of the information presented as true and accurate. The capacity to lie with a picture and be undetected has been greatly increased by modern computer technology.

SECTION 6
Hypnosis and
"Reefer Madness"

MIND CONTROL IS BEING USED ON AN UNSUSPECTING PUBLIC. MIND CONTROL IS BEING USED ON AN UNSUSPECTING PUBLIC.
MIND CONTROL IS BEING USED ON AN UNSUSPECTING PUBLIC. MIND CONTROL IS BEING USED ON AN UNSUSPECTING PUBLIC.
MIND CONTROL IS BEING USED ON AN UNSUSPECTING PUBLIC. MIND CONTROL IS BEING USED ON AN UNSUSPECTING PUBLIC.
MIND CONTROL IS BEING USED ON AN UNSUSPECTING PUBLIC. MIND CONTROL IS BEING USED ON AN UNSUSPECTING PUBLIC.

The power of hypnosis is the power of suggestion. The power of suggestion is the power of belief. It is an act of faith. The conscious mind cannot be controlled by the suggestions of someone else when those suggestions are contrary to what you know from your own experience. But the subconscious mind is susceptible to control by suggestion.[35] The subconscious mind has absolute control of the functions, conditions, and sensations of the body. Perfect anesthesia can be produced by suggestion. Hundreds of cases are recorded where surgical operations have been performed without pain to patients under hypnosis. Symptoms of almost any disease can be induced in hypnotic subjects by suggestions. Partial or total paralysis can be produced; fever can be brought on, with all the attendant symptoms such as rapid pulse and high temperature.[36]

In 1936, a movie used hypnotic suggestion to give the audience instructions to do something. That movie was *Reefer Madness*. Shown widely on college campuses and at midnight screenings across the country since 1972, *Reefer Madness* uses sophisticated hypnotic techniques to both encourage marijuana use and promote anti-marijuana legislation.

Speaking to a PTA meeting, high school principal Dr. Carroll commands parents to stamp out this "assassin of our youth"–marijuana. When Dr. Carroll begins to speak, he raises a sheet of paper in front of him and reads certain "facts" from it. The white sheet of paper prominent in the middle of the screen is a distraction for the eyes to cause that state of mind that is just like "day dreaming" while information is programmed to the audience verbally. Dr. James Braid discovered that by placing a bright object before the eyes of the subject, and causing him to gaze upon it with persistent attention, he could be led into the hypnotic state of mind.[37] Dr. Carroll delivers his lines with a hypnotic rhythm that is punctuated by changes in pacing, volume and tone (just like a hypnotist). Dr. Carroll speaks with authority. This happens to be a technique used in hypnosis. Authoritarian techniques, sometimes called paternal techniques, use a strong, commanding, dominating approach.[38] Dr. Carroll looks into the camera and into the eyes of the audience, another hypnotic technique. Picture yourself in a movie theatre, now imagine a huge face on the screen staring at you.

Other hypnotic techniques used in *Reefer Madness* include two-frame flashes in different places in the movie. These flash frames produce a corresponding wave in the brain. These flash frames "anchor" information from the sound track to your mind. These flash frames add emphasis to information on the sound track, making that information more important. Dr. Carroll slams his fist on the desk frequently to emphasize a point. This sudden burst of sound "anchors" information to your mind. The added sound cue makes the information important. There is even a scene with a swinging hypnotic pendulum!

The stated intent of *Reefer Madness* was to stamp out the menace of marijuana because it leads to "acts of shocking violence, ending often in incurable insanity." In contrast, young people are shown having a good time smoking marijuana, partying, dancing, kissing and retreating to the bedroom. By showing young people having a good time smoking marijuana, *Reefer Madness* encourages young people to at least try it. By confusing marijuana with heroin and by telling the story of normal kids going berserk because of marijuana, *Reefer Madness* scares older people into demanding that something be done. Why are there conflicting messages in the movie? Why was hypnosis used in this movie and with such a high level of sophistication? The answers are within the movie.

"You government men have got to find some way to put an end to it," demands Dr. Carroll. The government man replies: "Of course, I agree with you Dr. Carroll. But do you realize that marihuana is not like other forms of DOPE. You see, it grows wild in almost every state of the union. Therefore, there is practically no inter-state commerce in the drug. As a result, the government's hands are tied. And frankly, the only sure cure is a wide-spread campaign in education." Some words trigger strong emotional responses in people. The word DOPE is one of them. This word is emphasized on the sound track. Though we are told that marijuana is not like other forms of "dope," the association is established.

Harry Anslinger was the first U.S. Commissioner of Narcotics, a position he held for 32 years; and was U.S. Representative on the United Nations Commission on Narcotic Drugs. In his book *The Murderers*, he wrote about his campaign against marijuana: "By 1937, under my direction, the bureau launched two important steps: first, a legislative plan to seek from Congress a new law that would place marihuana and its distribution directly under federal control. Secondly, on radio and at major forums... I told of this evil weed of the fields and riverbeds and roadsides. I wrote articles for magazines; our agents gave hundreds of lectures to parents, educators, social and civic leaders. In network broadcasts I reported on the growing list of crime, including murder and rape."

One of the articles Harry Anslinger wrote appeared in the July 1937 issue of *The American Magazine* titled "Marihuana—Assassin of Youth." There are striking similarities between the content of this article and the content of the movie *Reefer Madness*. For example, from the article: "In 1931, the marijuana file of the United States Narcotic Bureau was less than two inches thick, while today the reports crowd many large cabinets." Now compare this to what appeared in the movie. Dr. Carroll is with the government man who says: "Let me show you something. In 1930, the records on marijuana in the Washington office of the Narcotics Division scarcely filled a small folder like this (less than two inches thick). Today, they fill cabinets." The camera shows us a wall lined with file cabinets.

In the book *Outsiders*, Howard S. Becker describes how the Federal Bureau of Narcotics under Harry Anslinger created the marijuana problem to cause the public to demand legislation.[39] A bill giving the federal government control over marijuana was introduced in Congress by Representative Robert L. Doughton of North Carolina, Chairman of the House Ways and Means Committee.[40] On August 2, 1937, Franklin Delano Roosevelt signed into law the Marijuana Tax Act, which became effective on October 1, 1937.[41]

The purpose of propaganda is to direct public attention to certain "facts." "The whole art consists in doing this so skillfully that everyone will be convinced that the fact is real," writes Adolf Hitler in *Mein Kampf*. He describes the principles of effective propaganda: it must be aimed at the emotions; it must be limited to a few points; it must repeat those points over and over again until the public believes it. To be effective, propaganda must constantly short-circuit all thought and decision. It must operate on the individual subconsciously.[42] The principles behind *The Big Lie* of propaganda are the same principles of mind control, hypnotic suggestion, mental programming: distraction and repetition. With propaganda, distraction draws attention away from information that is true and directs attention to information that is false. Repetition of the false information imbeds it in your subconscious mind so that your acceptance of its truth becomes a conditioned response. You accept this information as true without thinking whenever it is presented to you again.

There is a vast amount of misinformation about marijuana, much of it originating in the 1930s with the so-called "educational campaign" of the Federal Bureau of Narcotics. Propaganda is not only meant to influence opinions and attitudes but also to cause action. Government propaganda "suggests" that public opinion demands what the government has already decided to do.[43] The official reasons given by the Federal Bureau of Narcotics for its opposition to the use of marijuana shifted completely during 1949-1950 from the claim that use of marijuana led to crime and violence to the claim that marijuana use led to heroin use.[44] When questioned by Congressman John Dingell of Michigan during testimony before the House Ways and Means Committee whether "the marijuana addict graduates into a heroin, an opium, or a cocaine user," Commissioner Anslinger replied: "No, Sir; I have not heard of a case of that kind."[45] However, in 1955, Anslinger appeared before a Senate subcommittee investigating the traffic in illicit drugs and testified that marijuana leads to heroin addiction.[46]

During Congressional hearings in 1937, Dr. W. C. Woodward, Legislative Counsel for the American Medical Association, pointed out that there was no competent primary evidence to support the claims against marijuana, only newspaper accounts about growing marijuana addiction and that marijuana causes crime.[47] These "news" accounts were "planted" by the Federal Bureau of Narcotics. Of seventeen articles condemning marijuana that appeared in popular magazines from July 1937 to June 1939, ten either acknowledged the help of the Bureau in furnishing facts and figures or gave evidence of having received help by using facts and figures that had appeared in Bureau publications or in testimony given during Congressional hearings. An indication of the Bureau's influence in these articles is found in repeated "atrocity" stories that were first reported by the Bureau.[48] These same stories appeared in *Reefer Madness*.

COMMENTARY: The Hegelian Dialectic is a method for bringing about change in a three-step process. This strategy is used in the so-called War on Drugs, the War on Terrorism, the War on Crime, etc. The first step is to create a problem. The second step is to create opposition to the problem – an opposing force that will serve as a catalyst for action. The third step is to offer a solution that will lead to a predetermined goal, thus bringing about change that would have been impossible to impose on people without proper psychological conditioning. By causing emotional stress and mental confusion, judgement is impaired and suggestibility increased. Under these conditions, people allow their rights to be diminished for the promise of security. It is a classic example of "crisis management" to bring about change.

MIND CONTROL IS BEING USED ON AN UNSUSPECTING PUBLIC. MIND CONTROL IS BEING USED ON AN UNSUSPECTING PUBLIC.
MIND CONTROL IS BEING USED ON AN UNSUSPECTING PUBLIC. MIND CONTROL IS BEING USED ON AN UNSUSPECTING PUBLIC.
MIND CONTROL IS BEING USED ON AN UNSUSPECTING PUBLIC. MIND CONTROL IS BEING USED ON AN UNSUSPECTING PUBLIC.
MIND CONTROL IS BEING USED ON AN UNSUSPECTING PUBLIC. MIND CONTROL IS BEING USED ON AN UNSUSPECTING PUBLIC.
MIND CONTROL IS BEING USED ON AN UNSUSPECTING PUBLIC. MIND CONTROL IS BEING USED ON AN UNSUSPECTING PUBLIC.
MIND CONTROL IS BEING USED ON AN UNSUSPECTING PUBLIC. MIND CONTROL IS BEING USED ON AN UNSUSPECTING PUBLIC.
MIND CONTROL IS BEING USED ON AN UNSUSPECTING PUBLIC. MIND CONTROL IS BEING USED ON AN UNSUSPECTING PUBLIC.
MIND CONTROL IS BEING USED ON AN UNSUSPECTING PUBLIC. MIND CONTROL IS BEING USED ON AN UNSUSPECTING PUBLIC.
MIND CONTROL IS BEING USED ON AN UNSUSPECTING PUBLIC. MIND CONTROL IS BEING USED ON AN UNSUSPECTING PUBLIC.
MIND CONTROL IS BEING USED ON AN UNSUSPECTING PUBLIC. MIND CONTROL IS BEING USED ON AN UNSUSPECTING PUBLIC.
MIND CONTROL IS BEING USED ON AN UNSUSPECTING PUBLIC. MIND CONTROL IS BEING USED ON AN UNSUSPECTING PUBLIC.
MIND CONTROL IS BEING USED ON AN UNSUSPECTING PUBLIC. MIND CONTROL IS BEING USED ON AN UNSUSPECTING PUBLIC.
MIND CONTROL IS BEING USED ON AN UNSUSPECTING PUBLIC. MIND CONTROL IS BEING USED ON AN UNSUSPECTING PUBLIC.
MIND CONTROL IS BEING USED ON AN UNSUSPECTING PUBLIC. MIND CONTROL IS BEING USED ON AN UNSUSPECTING PUBLIC.
MIND CONTROL IS BEING USED ON AN UNSUSPECTING PUBLIC. MIND CONTROL IS BEING USED ON AN UNSUSPECTING PUBLIC.
MIND CONTROL IS BEING USED ON AN UNSUSPECTING PUBLIC. MIND CONTROL IS BEING USED ON AN UNSUSPECTING PUBLIC.
MIND CONTROL IS BEING USED ON AN UNSUSPECTING PUBLIC. MIND CONTROL IS BEING USED ON AN UNSUSPECTING PUBLIC.
MIND CONTROL IS BEING USED ON AN UNSUSPECTING PUBLIC. MIND CONTROL IS BEING USED ON AN UNSUSPECTING PUBLIC.

SECTION 7
Information Control

By clever manipulation, people can be led to believe something that is not true when such information is carefully timed and presented by an accepted and respected authority. Information is processed by the brain in a very specific way. At the base of the brain, there is a "check valve" called the Reticular Activating System that screens information. What seems to happen is this: when new information is introduced, it is compared with previously acquired information and then catalogued. When the information is required, it is retrieved and brought into conscious awareness according to need. Now if there is no "file" for the piece of information, a file is begun and added to when related information is acquired. If you accept the information as true, it is catalogued that way. And if you reject the information as false, it is catalogued that way. However, if you don't know if the information is true or not, your trust in the source of information determines whether or not you accept it, even if you are not sure or don't understand it.

Secret knowledge is the basis of all power. Your source of information depends upon who you are and what position you hold in society. Your source of information determines the reliability of what you know. What you know and the reliability of what you know determines everything that happens to you. And information can be controlled. Words can inform or misinform. What people think can be controlled by controlling information. In Orwell's *1984*, the primary means of oppression is the absolute control of information. All published material is constantly changed so that history fulfills the wishes and aims of the government. "Who controls the past," ran the Party slogan, "controls the future: who controls the present controls the past."

In the book *Brainwashing in the High Schools*, E. Merrill Root examines eleven American history textbooks used in the Evanston Township High School in Evanston, Illinois from 1950 to 1952.[49] None of these textbooks makes it clear that the government of the United States is not a democracy but a republic. The Founding Fathers defined the form of government which they set up as a constitutional republic.[50] Not one of these textbooks lists the word "republic" in its index.[51] These textbooks interpret U.S. history primarily as a clash between rich and poor, haves and have-nots, "privileged" and "unprivileged," which is economic determinism, the essence of Marxism, where the triumph of "the common man" is progress towards a more perfect "people's democracy."[52] A trend shared by each of the textbooks reviewed was advocacy of a world government where global commitment is preferable to national interests, thus promoting world socialism and "Big" government.[53]

The college textbook *Introductory Psychology* (second edition) by Jonathan L. Freedman, published by Addison-Wesley Publishing Company, contains information that is misleading, contradictory and false. This book uses the principles of mental programming to program the student to accept information that is not true. This text was used for "General Psychology" course 221 at the University of North Carolina at Greensboro, fall semester, 1982.

This book defines hypnosis as "A state of consciousness produced by entrusting oneself to another person, and characterized by heightened suggestibility, acceptance of distortion, selective attention and similar symptoms."[54] Part of this definition is true, the rest is misleading and false. First of all, it is not necessary to entrust yourself to another person to produce the hypnotic state of mind. Dr. James Braid demonstrated that the hypnotic state of mind could be produced by fixing your gaze upon a bright object.[55] In fact, any repeating light or sound pattern can lead you into that state of mind that is just like "day dreaming." There is selective attention and heightened suggestibility. There is "acceptance of distortion" only when distorted information is given and you don't know that it is distorted information. The word "symptoms" is usually used when referring to an illness or disorder. The hypnotic state of mind is a natural state of mind; it is neither an illness nor a disorder. This book ends its discussion of hypnosis saying: "Although there is little evidence that anyone has used hypnosis for evil or unpleasant purposes, the potential for such may exist."[56]

U.S. intelligence officer Charles McQuiston says that Sirhan Sirhan was hypnotically programmed to kill Robert Kennedy.[57] Dr. John W. Heisse, Jr., president of the International Society of Stress Analysis, studied Sirhan's psychiatric charts and interviews. He believes that Sirhan was brainwashed under hypnosis: "Sirhan kept repeating certain phrases. This clearly revealed he had been programmed to put himself into a trance."[58] "It's very possible to distort and change somebody's mind through a number of hypnotic sessions," says Dr. Herbert Spiegel, a medical expert on hypnosis. "It can be described as brainwashing because the mind is cleared of its old emotions and values which are replaced by implanting other suggestions."[59] Behavior-modified agents, known as "zombies" in the intelligence community, are individuals who have been subconsciously programmed for a task.[60]

Here is what the second edition of *Introductory Psychology* says about brainwashing: "... some people who talk about brainwashing seem to believe that it involves extremely powerful methods that are almost irresistible. However, there is no evidence to suggest the existence of any such methods... in fact, the attempts at brainwashing that we know about were not especially successful."[61] It is interesting to note that, while more papers have been published on subliminal perception than on many other single topics in psychology, the space given the subject in most general textbooks is minimal to non-existent.[62]

"A general state education is a mere contrivance for molding people to be exactly like one another; and as the mold in which it casts them is that which pleases the predominant power in the government,... it establishes a despotism over the mind, leading by natural tendency to one over the body," said John Stuart Mills.[63] Education of the young is used to condition them to what comes later, thus eliminating the difference between propaganda and teaching.[64] Propaganda cannot work effectively without education. The mind is conditioned with vast amounts of information posing as "facts" and "knowledge" dispensed for ulterior motives.[65] The "educated" and "intellectuals" are the most vulnerable to propaganda because they absorb the largest amount of secondhand information and consider themselves to be "above" the effects of propaganda.[66]

The August 22, 1982 edition of the *Winston-Salem Journal* contains a story from the N.Y. Times News Service titled *Some Experts Doubt the Power of Subliminal Messages*: "Amid claims and counterclaims for the power and pervasiveness of subliminal techniques, little scientific evidence has accumulated to show that either exists... A number of psychologists are now challenging the very notion that people can be influenced in any way by messages they cannot consciously see or hear." *Remember that propaganda draws attention away from information that is true and directs attention to information that is false. Also remember that your trust in the source of your information determines whether or not you accept the information as true even if you are not sure or don't understand it.* Thomas Jefferson said: "The man who never looks into a newspaper is better informed than he who reads them, inasmuch as he who knows nothing is nearer the truth than he whose mind is filled with falsehoods and errors."[67] The article ends by quoting Charles F. Adams speaking for the American Association of Advertising Agencies in 1981: "We are convinced that there is no subliminal advertising in America today."[68]

Every major advertising agency in North America has sponsored extensive research into subliminal perception.[69] Vance Packard's 1957 book *The Hidden Persuaders* revealed that American industry was researching the use of subliminal messages to motivate people to buy their products. Wilson Bryan Key has written three books exposing the widespread and sophisticated use of subliminal ads by the advertising industry.[70] Even children are exploited for profit. "When you sell a kid on your product, if he can't get it, he will throw himself on the floor, stamp his feet, and cry. You can't get a reaction like that out of an adult."[71] Research on children begins as early as ages two and three using the psychological techniques of finger sensors, eye-tracking and brainwave measurements.[72] U.S. advertising agencies have exported commercial subliminal techniques throughout Western Europe, the Far East, and Latin America.[73] It is interesting to note that J. Walter Thompson, at one time the world's largest advertising agency, was the former employer of H. R. Haldeman and a half-dozen implicated Nixon White House aides during the Watergate scandal.[74]

COMMENTARY: The first objective of the commercial advertiser or the government propagandist is to create the conditions that will produce a state of mind favorable to receiving their message. That state is the hypnotic state and television is capable of inducing this altered state of consciousness automatically, regardless of the program content, due to the nature of the medium itself. This makes television the most potent instrument of mass persuasion in the history of the world.

MIND CONTROL IS BEING USED ON AN UNSUSPECTING PUBLIC. MIND CONTROL IS BEING USED ON AN UNSUSPECTING PUBLIC.
MIND CONTROL IS BEING USED ON AN UNSUSPECTING PUBLIC. MIND CONTROL IS BEING USED ON AN UNSUSPECTING PUBLIC.
MIND CONTROL IS BEING USED ON AN UNSUSPECTING PUBLIC. MIND CONTROL IS BEING USED ON AN UNSUSPECTING PUBLIC.
MIND CONTROL IS BEING USED ON AN UNSUSPECTING PUBLIC. MIND CONTROL IS BEING USED ON AN UNSUSPECTING PUBLIC.
MIND CONTROL IS BEING USED ON AN UNSUSPECTING PUBLIC. MIND CONTROL IS BEING USED ON AN UNSUSPECTING PUBLIC.

SECTION 8
Manipulation of Language

MIND CONTROL IS BEING USED ON AN UNSUSPECTING PUBLIC. MIND CONTROL IS BEING USED ON AN UNSUSPECTING PUBLIC.
MIND CONTROL IS BEING USED ON AN UNSUSPECTING PUBLIC. MIND CONTROL IS BEING USED ON AN UNSUSPECTING PUBLIC.
MIND CONTROL IS BEING USED ON AN UNSUSPECTING PUBLIC. MIND CONTROL IS BEING USED ON AN UNSUSPECTING PUBLIC.
MIND CONTROL IS BEING USED ON AN UNSUSPECTING PUBLIC. MIND CONTROL IS BEING USED ON AN UNSUSPECTING PUBLIC.
MIND CONTROL IS BEING USED ON AN UNSUSPECTING PUBLIC. MIND CONTROL IS BEING USED ON AN UNSUSPECTING PUBLIC.

In Orwell's *1984*, the manipulation of language is the key to controlling the people. In time, a new language is created so that the aims of the ruling elite might best be served. "Newspeak" redefines words that at one time had universal meaning, making it more and more difficult and ultimately impossible for people to communicate thoughts not sanctioned by the government. Traditional definitions are eliminated while new meanings are repeated over and over again until accepted. Language is used to conceal truth and dignify absurdities. In addition to debasing language, the principle of "doublethink" is instituted. Doublethink is the ability to accept two contradictory beliefs, without perceiving it is illogical to do so. "In the end the Party would announce that two and two made five, and you would have to believe it. It was inevitable that they should make that claim sooner or later: the logic of their position demanded it."

The Vietnam War produced many examples of government Newspeak and doublethink. Bombing missions were called "protective reaction strikes," a refugee camp became a "new life hamlet," and the American invasion of Cambodia was termed an "incursion." During the Nixon administration, government Newspeak and double think were rampant. When White House press secretary Ron Ziegler contradicted statements made previously, he termed his former statements "inoperative." Criminal acts were committed under the guise of "national security" and "executive privilege." Nixon aides abused their power from an "excess of zeal." As in *1984*, lies were the truth, the truth was a lie.[75] The February 11, 1984 edition of the *Winston-Salem Journal* contains a story from United Press International titled "State Department Strikes 'Killing' From Reports": "The word 'killing' has been stricken from State Department human rights reports. Officials explained yesterday that the government considers it more precise to say 'unlawful or arbitrary deprivation of life.' "[76]

The January 1984 edition of *Reader's Digest* contains an article titled "1984 Is Here: Where is Big Brother?" "Many would have us believe that George Orwell's classic novel *1984* is in fact a portrait of present-day America. Nonsense!"[77] The December 10, 1983 edition of *The Sentinel* contains an article by Edwin M. Yoder, Jr. of the Washington Post Writers Group titled '*1984* —Fantasy Year Could Never Be Otherwise': ". . . none of Orwell's imaginary nightmare materialized... the nightmare of total human conditioning remains but an ominous fantasy."[78] From *1984*: "The Party told you to reject the evidence of your eyes and ears. It was their final, most essential command."

Common sense tells us that one must first gain the confidence and respect of people in order to deceive them. "We frequently have the illusion that we are in complete control of ourselves and the contents of our minds and psyches; and it is this illusion that makes it possible for us to be manipulated all the more successfully."[79] Most people do not exercise their intelligence and critical faculties in evaluating the vast amount of information they are assaulted with. As a result, they abdicate their responsibility for what happens to them. However, responsibility cannot be discarded so easily and without a price to pay. "Those who expect to reap the blessings of freedom must, like men, undergo the fatigue of supporting it," wrote Thomas Paine.[80] Once freedom is lost, it is much harder to regain. History shows that when people do not take responsibility for their lives, there are those who will take it for them, and ultimately from them.

COMMENTARY: The essence of psychological warfare is to confuse the meaning of words and infiltrate the mind with conflicting concepts. The manipulation of words and their meaning is the key to controlling what people think. Orwell called the redefining of words "Newspeak," where *traditional* definitions are eliminated while *new* meanings are repeated over and over again until accepted. Words create reality. Words have tangible, long-lasting effects on our lives. The political concepts of the United States have undergone a gradual alteration through the manipulation of words and their meaning. Government and society are changed by changing words and their definition.

Here are some other examples to ponder: Use of the word "Federal" in the name "Federal Reserve" leads the public to believe that the Federal Reserve is a government institution. Contrary to this misleading use of language, the FED is a private corporation owned by foreign and domestic banks and operated for profit. The definition of the word "dollar" has undergone a transformation to hide the fact that it is not money, but a unit of measure for gold and silver coin. Gold and silver coin were taken out of circulation, removed as backing for our currency, and replaced with monetized debt – in other words, credit. Credit exists only in the mind. It is not a substance that can be weighed and measured, but an idea represented by bookkeeping entries and computer symbols. It is entirely psychological.

A dollar is not money. A dollar is a unit of measurement like an inch or a quart or a mile. If there are no gold and silver coins, there are no dollars of anything! Dollars cannot be money any more than quarts can be milk. A unit of measurement cannot replace or become the "thing" for which it is the measure. However, in the mind of the public, this is exactly what has happened. People have been led to believe that a dollar is both money and a measure of it. This is what Orwelll called "double-think" and what the Bible calls being "double-minded," where the mind is infiltrated with conflicting concepts without being aware of it. The money system operates in a way that would astound most Americans if they only knew how it worked. A dishonest money system is at the very heart of America's economic and social problems. The degree to which the money system is corrupt is the degree to which all other areas of society are corrupted.

MIND CONTROL IS BEING USED ON AN UNSUSPECTING PUBLIC. MIND CONTROL IS BEING USED ON AN UNSUSPECTING PUBLIC.
MIND CONTROL IS BEING USED ON AN UNSUSPECTING PUBLIC. MIND CONTROL IS BEING USED ON AN UNSUSPECTING PUBLIC.
MIND CONTROL IS BEING USED ON AN UNSUSPECTING PUBLIC. MIND CONTROL IS BEING USED ON AN UNSUSPECTING PUBLIC.
MIND CONTROL IS BEING USED ON AN UNSUSPECTING PUBLIC. MIND CONTROL IS BEING USED ON AN UNSUSPECTING PUBLIC.
MIND CONTROL IS BEING USED ON AN UNSUSPECTING PUBLIC. MIND CONTROL IS BEING USED ON AN UNSUSPECTING PUBLIC.
MIND CONTROL IS BEING USED ON AN UNSUSPECTING PUBLIC. MIND CONTROL IS BEING USED ON AN UNSUSPECTING PUBLIC.
MIND CONTROL IS BEING USED ON AN UNS   BEING USED ON AN UNSUSPECTING PUBLIC.
MIND CONTROL IS BEING USED ON AN UNS   BEING USED ON AN UNSUSPECTING PUBLIC.
MIND CONTROL IS BEING USED ON AN UNS   BEING USED ON AN UNSUSPECTING PUBLIC.
MIND CONTROL IS BEING USED ON AN UNSUSPECTING PUBLIC. MIND CONTROL IS BEING USED ON AN UNSUSPECTING PUBLIC.
MIND CONTROL   PECTING PUBLIC.
MIND CONTROL   PECTING PUBLIC.
MIND CONTROL   PECTING PUBLIC.
MIND CONTROL IS BEING USED ON AN UNSUSPECTING PUBLIC. MIND CONTROL IS BEING USED ON AN UNSUSPECTING PUBLIC.
MIND CONTROL IS BEING USED ON AN UNSUSPECTING PUBLIC. MIND CONTROL IS BEING USED ON AN UNSUSPECTING PUBLIC.
MIND CONTROL IS BEING USED ON AN UNSUSPECTING PUBLIC. MIND CONTROL IS BEING USED ON AN UNSUSPECTING PUBLIC.
MIND CONTROL IS BEING USED ON AN UNSUSPECTING PUBLIC. MIND CONTROL IS BEING USED ON AN UNSUSPECTING PUBLIC.
MIND CONTROL IS BEING USED ON AN UNSUSPECTING PUBLIC. MIND CONTROL IS BEING USED ON AN UNSUSPECTING PUBLIC.

SECTION 9
Monopoly of Mass Media

"The nearly complete monopoly of mass communications is generally agreed to be one of the most striking characteristics of totalitarian dictatorships," writes President Carter's National Security Adviser Zbigniew Brzezinski in his book *Totalitarian Dictatorship and Autocracy*. Brzezinski goes on to say that even though the government controls all the means of communication in a dictatorship, the government doesn't necessarily have to own all the means of communication.[81] Without mass media, there could be no effective propaganda. To make the coordination of propaganda possible, the media must be concentrated, the number of news agencies reduced, and press, publishing, radio, television and film monopolies established.[82] Only through concentration in a few hands of a large number of media can there be an orchestration and continuity to propaganda and the application of scientific methods to influence the public.[83] The campaign against marijuana that led to the Marijuana Tax Act illustrates such co-ordination of the media and psychological manipulation.

The motion picture industry is a prime example of the tendency toward concentration of ownership in the communications media. From its beginning, the film industry has been characterized by repeated attempts at domination by a small number of companies that traditionally have tried either to exclude others from the business or to deprive competitors of resources.[84] Dominance in the American market is carried abroad by the major companies and has cultural, social and political consequences.[85] The desire for American goods in other countries was created by American films. After World War II, the film industry and the government worked together for world-wide distribution to create markets for American goods.[86] U.S. made films account for half the box office receipts in France and more in

England, West Germany and elsewhere. Eddie Murphy was "actor of the year" for the Paris daily *Le Matin*, Michael Jackson was top singer. European radios play up to eighty percent American music. Each week "Starsky and Hutch" speak street Parisian to Huggy Bear. Magnum, the Harts and Charlie's Angels are only a few of Europe's television heroes. In Iceland, "Soap" was the top show of 1983. "We have colonized their subconscious," observes American novelist Paul Theroux.[87] Hypnotically programming large populations, especially in economically underdeveloped nations, educates the poor to want things that they cannot realistically have, causing anxiety and resentment directed not only to their government but to the United States as well. Many countries are rebelling against this cultural invasion by the American media. "At U.S. bases in Germany, people protest missiles while wearing Coca-Cola T-shirts," says Alfred Mechtersheimer of the Institute for Peace Politics near Munich.[88]

The 1940 Republican Presidential candidate Wendell L. Wilkie was chairman of the board of Twentieth Century-Fox Film Corp. in 1942.[89] William P. Rogers, Secretary of State during the Nixon administration, was on the board of directors of Twentieth Century-Fox before Denver oil tycoon Marvin Davis bought the film company for $722 million in June 1981.[90] Former President Gerald R. Ford and Henry Kissinger have both been on the board of directors of Twentieth Century-Fox and consultants to the film company.[91] In 1982, Henry Kissinger became a consultant for ABC News and was a consultant for NBC in 1977.[92] Former Vice President Walter F. Mondale was a member of the board of directors of Columbia Pictures Industries before the Atlanta-based Coca-Cola Company bought Columbia Pictures in June 1982 for $751.6 million.[93] And former Secretary of State Alexander M. Haig, Jr. was on the board of directors of MGM/UA Entertainment Company.[94]

COMMENTARY: There could be no effective propaganda without mass media. Former national editor at *The Washington Post* and Dean of the Graduate School of Journalism at the University of California at Berkeley, Ben Bagdikian reported in his book *The Media Monopoly* published in 1983, that fifty corporations controlled most of America's media. When the second edition of the book was published in 1988, that number shrank to twenty-nine. In the third edition published in 1990, the number shrank further to twenty-six. Today it is just a handful. The consolidation of ownership of the press, publishing, radio, television and film makes the coordination of propaganda possible. The problem is that the media is controlled by corporations that are controlled by the super-rich who have a vested interest in keeping the public in a trance, ignorant, anxious, fearful, highly suggestible and vulnerable to control and manipulation. The nation is experiencing the effects of a scientifically induced nervous breakdown. Psychological warfare and economic warfare are both being used against an unsuspecting public. The nation has been placed in a vise and is being squeeeeeezed, causing agitation, stress, anxiety, fear, anger and frustration. On one end of the vise is the mass media which is used to program, propagandize, badger and wear down the public emotionally with negative images and stories. On the other end of the vise is the manipulation of the economy to cause added stress so that people do not know if they are coming or going. No wonder people cannot think clearly or be peaceful! All this creates a dull-mindedness and trance-like state in the population while the nation is looted and Constitutional and human rights are ignored and trampled.

MIND CONTROL IS BEING USED ON AN UNSUSPECTING PUBLIC. MIND CONTROL IS BEING USED ON AN UNSUSPECTING PUBLIC.
MIND CONTROL IS BEING USED ON AN UNSUSPECTING PUBLIC. MIND CONTROL IS BEING USED ON AN UNSUSPECTING PUBLIC.
MIND CONTROL IS BEING USED ON AN UNSUSPECTING PUBLIC. MIND CONTROL IS BEING USED ON AN UNSUSPECTING PUBLIC.
MIND CONTROL IS BEING USED ON AN UNSUSPECTING PUBLIC. MIND CONTROL IS BEING USED ON AN UNSUSPECTING PUBLIC.
MIND CONTROL IS BEING USED ON AN UNSUSPECTING PUBLIC. MIND CONTROL IS BEING USED ON AN UNSUSPECTING PUBLIC.
MIND CONTROL IS BEING USED ON AN UNSUSPECTING PUBLIC. MIND CONTROL IS BEING USED ON AN UNSUSPECTING PUBLIC.
MIND CONTROL IS BEING USED ON AN UNSUSPECTING PUBLIC. MIND CONTROL IS BEING USED ON AN UNSUSPECTING PUBLIC.
MIND CONTROL IS BEING USED ON AN UNSUSPECTING PUBLIC. MIND CONTROL IS BEING USED ON AN UNSUSPECTING PUBLIC.
MIND CONTROL IS BEING USED ON AN UNSUSPECTING PUBLIC. MIND CONTROL IS BEING USED ON AN UNSUSPECTING PUBLIC.
MIND CONTROL IS BEING USED ON AN UNSUSPECTING PUBLIC. MIND CONTROL IS BEING USED ON AN UNSUSPECTING PUBLIC.
MIND CONTROL IS BEING USED ON AN UNSUSPECTING PUBLIC. MIND CONTROL IS BEING USED ON AN UNSUSPECTING PUBLIC.
MIND CONTROL IS BEING USED ON AN UNSUSPECTING PUBLIC. MIND CONTROL IS BEING USED ON AN UNSUSPECTING PUBLIC.
MIND CONTROL IS BEING USED ON AN UNSUSPECTING PUBLIC. MIND CONTROL IS BEING USED ON AN UNSUSPECTING PUBLIC.
MIND CONTROL IS BEING USED ON AN UNSUSPECTING PUBLIC. MIND CONTROL IS BEING USED ON AN UNSUSPECTING PUBLIC.
MIND CONTROL IS BEING USED ON AN UNSUSPECTING PUBLIC. MIND CONTROL IS BEING USED ON AN UNSUSPECTING PUBLIC.
MIND CONTROL IS BEING USED ON AN UNSUSPECTING PUBLIC. MIND CONTROL IS BEING USED ON AN UNSUSPECTING PUBLIC.

SECTION 10

Mental Programming

and Mass Media

Motion pictures were an effective propaganda weapon during both world wars. German Chief of Staff Erich Ludendorff, writing in 1917, said: "The war has demonstrated the superiority of the photograph and the film as a means of information and persuasion."[95] Lenin considered the cinema the most important of the arts. "Molding the feeling and intelligence of the masses is one of our political problems and for this end we find the movies most effective," said Russian film director Sergei Eisenstein.[96] Art is a way of seeing and what we see in art defines what we understand to be "reality." The great political problem of the United States at the end of the nineteenth century was to find a way to assimilate the vast numbers of people who came from all the countries of Europe bringing with them their diverse traditions. The solution was psychological standardization. This was accomplished by creating the American way of life as portrayed by the "American Dream." This also served an economic function. Mass production requires mass consumption. There cannot be mass consumption without the majority of the population having identical views about what constitutes the necessities of life. Without psychological uniformity advertising and other forms of propaganda could not manipulate the public with certainty.[97]

D. W. Griffith's *The Birth of a Nation* exploded on the screen in 1915 and caused dissension in almost every city and community it played.[98] The radio broadcast of *The War of the Worlds* caused panic. *Reefer Madness* encouraged marijuana use and was part of a propaganda campaign that led to the Marijuana Tax Act. *The Warriors*, one of a number of "gang" movies, was followed by a rash of violence in cities across the nation.[99]

Approximately twenty-eight people died playing Russian roulette in response to viewing *The Deer Hunter*. The press reported that John Hinkley, Jr. told his attorneys that the idea to assassinate President Ronald Wilson Reagan came to him after he saw *Taxi Driver*.[100] A report released in 1982 by the National Institute of Mental Health said "violence on television does lead to aggressive behavior by children and teenagers who watch the programs."[101]

ABC Motion Pictures president Brandon Stoddard called *The Day After* the most important movie ever made.[102] One of the most talked-about programs in television history, *The Day After* graphically depicts the devastation of Lawrence, Kansas in a thermonuclear apocalypse, the agonies of survivors and the breakdown of society where law-abiding citizens emerge from the rubble to loot, rape and pillage, broadcast weeks before the scheduled deployment of American Pershing II missiles in Western Europe. Produced on videotape for realism, the made-for-TV movie *Special Bulletin* about terrorists exploding an atomic bomb in Charleston, South Carolina looks and sounds like a real news broadcast in every detail. Like the radio broadcast of *The War of the Worlds*, the cast of characters include the anchorperson(s), correspondents reporting from the field and outside "experts" brought in to comment on new developments. Despite disclaimers, the re-run of *Special Bulletin* prompted numerous calls to stations across the nation from people who wanted to know if it was real.[103]

The techniques of psychotherapy, widely practiced and accepted as a means of curing psychological disorders, are also methods of controlling people. They can be used systematically to influence attitudes and behavior.[104] Systematic desensitization is a method used to dissolve anxiety so that the patient (public) is no longer troubled by a specific fear, a fear of violence for example.[105] A progressively more graphic depiction of violence in the movies and on television desensitizes the viewer, especially young people, to real-life violence. People adapt to frightening circumstances if they are exposed to them enough. Implosive therapy serves the same purpose as desensitization. However, instead of gradually wearing down a specific fear, this method is designed to create an internal explosion (implosion) of anxiety, frightening the patient (public) as much as possible to "burn out" the object of fear.[106] Thus, *The Day After* and *Special Bulletin* could leave many viewers so numbed by a sense of hopelessness and helplessness that they could succumb to deep apathy with regard to anything that has to do with the prospect of nuclear confrontation.

For anyone who saw *Close Encounters of the Third Kind*, who can forget the five-position hand gesture used by the extra-terrestrial being in greeting the human contingent at the landing base and the emotions that welled inside, a feeling of pride that we are somehow part of something that is much vaster than anything we have imagined. Communication depends heavily upon actions, postures, movements and expressions.[107] Think back to the times when you have had a conversation with someone and you had the "gut feeling" that you were being lied to. Words don't always communicate truthfully and there are things that communicate more than words. Meaning comes from the sound of someone's voice and "body language." There are many ways of "faking" body language to achieve an end. Authors of books on self-improvement and how to make friends and influence people are aware of the importance of body language and the importance of faking it properly to guarantee social success. Politicians have learned its importance and how to use it effectively. No matter what John Kennedy said, a few gestures and a correct posture captivated his audience.[108] Lyndon Johnson's arm motions were always too studied, too mannered. Nixon's gestures were so rigid and exaggerated that they lent themselves to a comic mimicry.[109] With his shirt sleeves rolled up, Jimmy Carter tried to show that he was at ease with ordinary people and said: "I will never lie to you; I will never mislead you." Contrary to the Carter image, one veteran speech writer left Carter's campaign: "The candidate and the campaign were the opposite of what they appeared to be."[110] NBC News reporter Roger Mudd made the observation that Senator Gary Hart seemed to imitate the late President Kennedy.[111] Rev. Jesse Jackson is an accomplished orator, speaking with an evangelistic tone, metaphor and rhyme. His hand gestures are deliberate and convey an emotional context to his words. It should not be forgotten that President Reagan had extensive training as an actor. Called "The Great Communicator" by the media, Ronald Reagan was a politician who is a "real" actor, a man who began his career by convincing radio audiences that he was at a sports event when in fact he was reading off a ticker-tape machine and inventing the details.[112]

Think for a moment about the way newscasters speak and you will realize that they all talk the same way regardless of their ethnic background. Whether they be black, white, hispanic or oriental, they all sound alike.

"News-speak" has become a language pattern associated with the dissemination of true, factual information. Consider the laugh tracks that have become an integral part of TV comedies. They "educate" the audience to "respond" to what is "funny."[113] The audience has been programmed to associate a resonating low monotone voice with evil because of the evil behavior of movie and television characters with that vocal quality. Emotions can be stirred, attitudes and states of mind revealed by nuances of tone and variation in vocal quality. The camera can reveal the smallest movement and the most subtle change of expression and give them significance and definition. Popular performers, past and present, are "role models" for the audience to admire and emulate, thus promoting a standard for behavior. The public has been programmed to accept stereotypes that categorize people and professions. All verbal and non-verbal communication has been identified, defined and reduced to a code that can be manipulated. Describing the incredible power of network television, Senator Gary Hart said: "It's a very frightening thing, if you think about it enough. A Hitler, a dictator, could rise in a matter of a few days with the proper use of TV. I think it could really happen."[114] It is possible to program an entire population to respond to certain words, images, vocal qualities, body movements, gestures and expressions with certainty. The result of such programming is a population that is highly suggestible, a population that can be manipulated with precision.

SECTION 11
The Power of Money

Conspiracies to seize the power of government are as old as the institution of government.[115] "In politics, nothing happens by accident. If it happens, you can bet it was planned that way," said Franklin Delano Roosevelt.[116] During the past two centuries when the peoples of the world were gradually winning political freedom from monarchies, the major banking families of Europe and America were reversing the trend by forming new dynasties of political control through international financial alliances.[117] The goal was to create a world-wide system of financial control in order to dominate the economy of the world and the political system of each country.[118]

The United States is dominated by a hierarchy of wealthy families.[119] The control of private wealth is held by families and family alliances, reinforced by marriages among their members, that guide the banks and control the corporations.[120] Historically, government has been the servant of private wealth.[121] The first fortunes in the New World were political creations. Land and trading privileges were granted by the British and Dutch crowns upon favored individuals and companies.[122] Every great fortune that came out of the nineteenth century was rooted in fraud. "In their absorbing passion for the accumulation of wealth, men were plundering the resources of the country like burglars looting a palace."[123] The public has been deluded about the material aims of a few and the very existence of those who rule the majority. Rule through money has been fashioned into the ultimate system for securing and maintaining power.[124]

Nineteenth century American author Edward Bellamy, concerned with the extent and consequences of man's inhumanity to man, describes how the "system" operates in *The Parable of The Water Tank*: There was a certain very dry land and the people needed water badly. They did nothing but look for water and many perished because they could not find any. There were, however, certain men in that land who were more cunning than the rest and they gathered supplies of water where others could find none, and these men were called capitalists. The people came unto the capitalists and begged for water and the capitalists answered: "Be ye our servants and ye shall have water." And so the capitalists organized the people and they made a great tank for the water, and the tank was called the Market. The capitalists said unto the people: "For every bucket of water that ye bring us, we will give you a penny, but for every bucket that we give unto you, ye shall give to us two pennies, and the difference shall be our profit, seeing that if it were not for this profit we would not do this thing for you and you would all perish." And after many days the water tank, which was the Market, did overflow and the capitalists said unto the people: "Bring us no more water till the tank be empty." But when the people received no more pennies from the capitalists, they could buy no more water. And when the capitalists saw that they had no more profit, they were troubled and said among themselves, "We must advertise." But the people had no pennies to buy the water and the situation was called a "crisis".

The thirst of the people was great, but the capitalists would not give of the water, saying "Business is business." But the capitalists were disturbed because the people bought no more water, and so they acquired no more profits. They then sent for the soothsayers to interpret this predicament. The soothsayers were men learned in dark sayings, who joined themselves to the capitalists so that they would have water, and they spoke for the capitalists and did their bidding for them. The soothsayers said that the people bought no more water because of "overproduction" and others said it was because of "lack of confidence." The capitalists were comforted and they sent the soothsayers unto the people who saw the emptiness of their wisdom and did mock them. The capitalists became fearful that the people would come upon the tank and take the water by force. And so they brought forth certain holy men who were false priests to testify to the people that this affliction was sent to them by God for the healing of their souls, and that if they would bear it in patience and lust not after the water, nor trouble the capitalists, it would come to pass that after they had given up the ghost they would come to a place where there would be no capitalists but an abundance of water.

When the capitalists saw that the people were still discontent and would not be still, neither for the words of the soothsayers nor of the false priests, they came forth themselves and wet their fingertips in the water that overflowed from the tank and they scattered the drops upon the people and the drops were called "charity." But still there was great unrest among the people. The capitalists sought out the mightiest and all who had skill in war and they became a defense unto the capitalists. And after many days the water was low in the tank, for the capitalists wasted the water for their pleasure. When the capitalists saw that the tank was empty, they said, "The crisis is ended." They hired the people to fill again the tank that was the Market, and gave the people a penny for each bucket the people brought and took two pennies for each bucket they did give unto the people.[125]

COMMENTARY: During the Middle Ages, it became common practice for people to store their gold in the vault of the local goldsmith for a fee. The goldsmith would give the depositor a receipt for the amount of gold stored for safekeeping. The receipt was not money, but a money *substitute*. It also became common practice for people to exchange these "warehouse receipts" with one another for goods and services as *if* they were money since the receipts could be redeemed for the gold held in storage. This is where the idea originates for bank checks and checking accounts.

The goldsmith soon discovered that only a small percentage of the gold stored in his vault was ever reclaimed at any one time. He began issuing receipts for more gold than he had on deposit in the vault, using some of them himself to buy things and loaning the rest at interest, while taking title to real property as collateral. In either case, there was no gold in the vault for these extra receipts. By increasing the quantity of the money *substitute*, the goldsmith had stolen from the holders of legitimate receipts, the value of which was reduced by the number of fraudulent receipts issued.

Paper currency, a money substitute, is honest only when the real money for which it is a substitute equals the number of receipts in circulation. By manipulating the number of receipts in circulation, the goldsmith quietly confiscated the wealth of the community without anyone being aware of what was happening. By reducing the number of receipts, he could make money scarce, causing a depression where he could foreclose on property and increase his wealth. He could then stimulate economic activity and bring prosperity by increasing the number of receipts until the next cycle of plunder. All of America's economic problems originate with the practice of issuing fraudulent receipts for gold that does not exist. This practice became standard operating procedure for the banking establishment.

The modern-day counterpart to the warehouse receipt for gold is the Federal Reserve Note. *Remember: the essence of psychological warfare is to confuse the meaning of words and infiltrate the mind with conflicting concepts.* The word "Federal" implies Federal Government, but the Federal Reserve is a privately-owned corporation. The word "Reserve" implies there is something to give the paper receipt value, but no gold or silver backs this paper. The word "Note" implies a contract, because a note by law must identify *who* is paying, *what* is being paid, *to whom* and *when.*

Can Paper Become What It Promises by Removing the Promise?

Between 1914 and 1963, Federal Reserve Notes never claimed to be money, nor did they claim to be dollars. A note for twenty dollars read as follows: "THE UNITED STATES OF AMERICA WILL PAY TO THE BEARER ON DEMAND TWENTY DOLLARS." Can a promise to pay twenty dollars *be* twenty dollars? To the left of the President's picture and above the bank seal, it said in small print: **"THIS NOTE IS LEGAL TENDER FOR ALL DEBTS, PUBLIC AND PRIVATE, AND IS REDEEMABLE IN LAWFUL MONEY AT THE UNITED STATES TREASURY, OR AT ANY FEDERAL RESERVE BANK."**

In 1963, soon after the assassination of President John F. Kennedy while the nation was still traumatized and in shock, the FED began to issue its first series of notes *without* the promise, while taking notes *with* the promise out of circulation. To the left of the President's picture and above the bank seal, it now read: **"THIS NOTE IS LEGAL TENDER FOR ALL DEBTS, PUBLIC AND PRIVATE."**

By *removing* the promise to redeem the note in lawful money, the Federal Government in cooperation with the Federal Reserve eliminated the monetary system of the United States established by the Constitution and replaced it with something *totally different*. A note is an IOU. It is evidence of debt. It is *not* possible to pay off a debt with a debt. The name "Federal Reserve Note" is a fraudulent label since each word claims to be something that in reality it is not.

On page 12 of *Keeping Our Money Healthy* published by the Federal Reserve Bank of New York, it states: *"the Federal Reserve System works only with credit."* Credit is not a tangible substance like gold or silver coin. You cannot touch it nor can you weigh or measure it in dollars like gold or silver coin. Credit exists only in the mind and it is necessary to control minds to induce the public to accept pieces of paper with numbers on them in place of lawful money. It is the responsibility of honest government to insure that the money system serve the nation and not enslave the nation. The money system has been fashioned into the ultimate system for securing and maintaining power. In fact, it is the ultimate slave system. All that it took to enslave the United States (and the world) was to convince people that paper and credit are money.

There are only two economic systems: one is barter; the other is credit. Barter is the exchange of one thing of value for something else of value. Throughout history, many different things have served as a medium of exchange because money, in and of itself, does not exist. Something must be used *as* money. People have traded for goods and services using livestock, salt, tea, opium and tobacco. Gold and silver have been accepted as money since ancient times. All things used as money have had a common characteristic: they were all *tangible* wealth. They were all things you could touch. They were all things you could weigh and measure. Credit, on the other hand, is intangible. You cannot touch it. You cannot weigh and measure it because there is no substance to weigh and measure. It is all imagination.

An honest money system uses wealth as a medium of exchange. Wealth is physical, not psychological. People produce wealth through their labor transforming natural resources into usable products that have exchange value in the marketplace. Gold and silver converted to coin by human labor is wealth. Credit is *not* wealth. No labor is expended in the creation of credit other than a magician's sleight of hand. Centuries ago, when the goldsmith issued his first receipt for gold that did not exist, he created credit. He also created inflation because credit and inflation are the same thing. They are both receipts for wealth that does not exist. They are both an imaginary medium of exchange. Remember paper currency, a money substitute, is *honest* only when the real money for which it is a substitute equals the number of receipts in circulation. When *half* of the receipts circulating as a money substitute are redeemable in gold, the other *half* is both credit and inflation. When *none* of the receipts are redeemable, *all* of it is credit and inflation.

An honest and sound money system employs just weights and measures. A ten dollar gold coin is twice as large and twice as heavy as a five dollar gold coin. Remember a dollar is a unit of measurement for gold and silver coin to insure uniformity of weight, purity and value. A dollar unit of paper money that is not one hundred percent redeemable in gold or silver coin is a dollar unit of inflation, which is a dollar unit of credit, which is a dollar unit of nothing. Daniel Webster said: *"Of all the contrivances devised for cheating the laboring classes of mankind, none has been more effective than that which deludes him with paper money."*

The only source of inflation is the Federal Reserve Banking System, consisting of the twelve Federal Reserve Banks dominated by the Federal Reserve Bank of New York and the nations commercial banks. Banks create money whenever they make a loan. Banks lend money that did not exist until they loaned it. It is the act of borrowing that causes it to come into existence. It is a true feat of magic. Banks create money by monetizing debt, the debts of government, business and the public. Banks literally create money out of less than nothing because a debt is a sum of money due. It is not possible to pay a debt with a debt, and yet this is what is being used as money! Increasing the amount of currency and checkbook money increases inflation. Creating new dollars reduces the value of all dollars, resulting in higher prices.

By manipulating the quantity of created dollars, the purchasing power of every dollar is altered. The expansion and contraction of an artificial money supply produces the cycles of prosperity and depression that have long plagued society. Depressions are the result of private bankers reducing the money supply by tightening credit and withdrawing currency, causing a drop in prices, unemployment and foreclosure of property. The absurdity of the situation is that if there were no debts, there would be no money, since every dollar of paper currency and checkbook money is loaned into circulation. And, in order to pay the interest, there has to be another loan because the banking system only creates the principal and not the interest. In fact, the interest can *never* be paid because it is not possible to return to the bank *more* dollars than were created, making it inevitable that the privately owned banking system acquire title to all wealth in the nation.

Credit, which is deferred payment and debt, which is a sum of money due, are the same thing, which is hidden by deceptive double-entry bookkeeping where a debt becomes an asset by calling it a credit. Paper money that redeems nothing only appears to have value because it can be exchanged for things of value. When a piece of paper representing debt is exchanged for wealth, someone has been robbed. Paper money expropriates wealth from one person, then from another, then from another, and on and on until the last person to get it will be stuck with it. The sole function of paper money that is not one hundred percent redeemable in gold or silver coin is to get things without paying for them. Those who issue and control bank credit as money get everything for nothing. Bank credit is a devise for confiscating wealth using magic with numbers where numbers of nothing are exchanged for things of substance and value. This grand theft occurs in full view unnoticed because the public has been made an accessory to the crime by accepting pieces of paper with numbers on them in place of lawful money, not knowing the difference between the two. The distinction between free men and slaves is whether or not they are paid for their labor. He who labors for money the first user got for nothing is a slave to the first user – the banks and their owners. There can be no liberty, no justice, no economic freedom without an honest money system.

SECTION 12
The Ruling Elite
and "World Government"

Nineteenth century British Prime Minister Benjamin Disraeli commented that the world is governed by very different people from what is imagined by those who are not behind the scenes. Dr. Carroll Quigley who taught at Harvard and Princeton and at the Foreign Service School of Georgetown University wrote about this network of "insiders" who govern from behind the scenes in *Tragedy and Hope—a History of the World In Our Time*: "I know of the operations of this network because I have studied it for twenty years and was permitted for two years, in the early 1960s, to examine its papers and secret instruments. I have objected, both in the past and recently, to a few of its policies (notably to its belief that England was an Atlantic rather than a European Power and must be allied, or even federated, with the United States and must remain isolated from Europe), but in general my chief difference of opinion is that it wishes to remain unknown, and I believe its role in history is significant enough to be known."[126]

Political and economic power in the United States is concentrated in the hands of a "ruling elite" that controls most U.S.-based multinational corporations, major communications media, the most influential foundations, major private universities and most public utilities.[127] Founded in 1921, the Council on Foreign Relations is the key link between the large corporations and the federal government.[128] It has been called a "school for statesmen" and "comes close to being an organ of what C. Wright Mills has called the Power Elite—a group of men, similar in interest and outlook shaping events from invulnerable positions behind the scenes."[129] The creation of the United Nations was a Council project, as well as the International Monetary Fund and the World Bank.[130] Council members

43

include Henry Kissinger, Gerald R. Ford, Jimmy Carter, Walter Mondale, Alexander Haig, George Schultz, Casper Weinberger.[131]

Twelve Council members were part of President Lyndon B. Johnson's Senior Advisory Group on Vietnam.[132] President Richard M. Nixon appointed more than 110 Council members to key government positions during his administration.[133] The majority of major appointments to the State Department by President Jimmy Carter in 1977 were members of the Council.[134] Most CIA directors have been Council members, including George Herbert Walker Bush and William Casey.[135] Nearly all major media in the U.S. have connections with the Council.[136] The president of the country's largest labor union, the AFL-CIO, Lane Kirkland was a member.[137] Membership includes a high concentration of corporate leaders from such companies as ITT, IBM and Standard Oil.[138] David Rockefeller has been a director of the Council since 1949 and chairman of the board since 1970.[139] The Council has been called "The Establishment," "the invisible government" and "the Rockefeller foreign office."[140] The goal of the Council is the establishment of a "World Government."[141]

Gold and diamond magnate Cecil Rhodes stated his commitment to the establishment of a World Government in his first will called the "Secret Society Will." His aim was clear: "The extension of British rule throughout the world." The secret society was called The Round Table, which worked behind the scenes at the highest levels of the British government. They organized Round Table Groups in those nations under British dominion and in the United States. In New York, it was known as the Council on Foreign Relations.[142] The *Chicago Tribune* editorial on December 9, 1950 states: "The members of the council are persons of much more than average influence in their community. They have used the prestige that their wealth, their social position, and their education have given them to lead this country toward bankruptcy and military debacle. They should look at their hands. There is blood on them—the dried blood of the last war and the fresh blood of the present one."[143] Administrations, both Democrat and Republican, change, but the Council on Foreign Relations remains.[144] The "insiders" control both the Democrat and Republican parties.[145]

There is, on the international level, an organization similar to the Council. This group calls itself the Bilderbergers, created by former Nazi SS storm trooper Prince Bernhard of the Netherlands.[146] Called "the most exclusive club of the Western establishment," the Bilderberg Group includes some of the world's most powerful financiers, industrialists, statesmen and intellectuals, who meet each year for a conference on world affairs.[147] Those attending have included British Prime Minister Margaret Thatcher, West German leader Helmut Schmidt, France's Valery Giscard D'Estaign, Henry Kissinger, Gerald R. Ford, Walter Mondale and David Rockefeller.[148] The ultimate goal of the Bilderberg Group is the establishment of a World Government.[149]

A World Government has always been the objective of Communism. The Bolshevik Revolution of November 1917 was a turning point in world history. "The main purveyors of funds for the revolution, however, were neither the crackpot Russian millionaires nor the armed bandits of Lenin. The "real" money primarily came from certain British and American circles which for a long time past had lent their support to the Russian revolutionary cause," writes General Arsene de Goulevitch in *Czarism and the Revolution*.[150]

Some of the world's richest and most powerful men financed the Bolshevik Revolution, a movement that claims it will strip these very same men of their power and wealth, men like the Rothschilds, Rockefellers, Schiffs, Warburgs, Morgans, Harrimans and Milners.[151] In *Decline of the West*, Oswald Spengler wrote: "There is no proletarian, not even a Communist movement, that has not operated in the interests of money, in the direction indicated by money, and for the time being permitted by money—and that without the idealists among its leaders having the slightest suspicion of the fact."[152] Describing events at the 1968 S.D.S national convention in *The Strawberry Statement: Notes of a College Revolutionary*, James Kunen says: "Also at the convention, men from Business International Roundtables—the meetings sponsored by Business International—tried to buy up a few radicals. These men are the world's leading industrialists and they convene to decide how our lives are going to go."[153]

The program of the Communist International of 1936 states that world dictatorship "can be established only by victory of socialism in different countries or groups of countries, after which the Proletariat Republics would unite on federal lines with those already in existence, and this system would expand...at length forming the world union of Soviet Socialist Republics."[154] Socialism means government ownership and/or control over the basic means of production and distribution of goods and services. State ownership and regulation of the entire economy means government control over everything. The evolution of economic history shows a straight line movement toward consolidation of wealth.[155] This evolution "flows from competition to combination, and from large combination to colossal combination, and it flows on to socialism, which is the most colossal combination of all."[156] Communism is totalitarian socialism. Communism is a movement created and manipulated by some of the world's most powerful and wealthy men in order to gain control over the world, first by establishing socialist governments in different countries and then consolidating them through a "Great Merger" into an all-powerful socialist dictatorship.[157]

John predicted that before the great epic of Millennial peace, humanity would be subjected to a ruthless, world-wide dictatorship which would attempt to make all men subservient to it or be killed (Revelation 13:15). He said that this dictatorship would compel men, "both small and great, rich and poor, free and bond," to be identified with it (Revelation 13:16). Unless a person be identified with its monopolistic control, "no man might buy and sell" (Revelation 13:17).

Founded in 1944 at a U.N. Monetary and Financial Conference at Bretton Woods, New Hampshire, the International Monetary Fund oversees the world economy. With its headquarters in Washington, the International Monetary Fund encourages financial cooperation between nations and lends money to governments which must comply with preconditions before the loans are granted. Dominated by Western nations, the International Monetary Fund manipulates the economies of industrialized nations and the developing countries. British economist Lord John Maynard Keynes envisioned it as the central world bank that would issue currency and control the world economy. Founded in 1944 along with the International Monetary Fund, the World Bank lends billions of dollars for economic development projects in underdeveloped countries, which must first join the International Monetary Fund before becoming eligible for World Bank aid. The Trilateral Commission, conceived by David Rockefeller, consists of an elite group of prominent business, political and intellectual leaders from Western Europe, North America and Japan. Members have included Jimmy Carter, Walter Mondale and George Bush. The Commission, established in 1973, promotes central management of the global economy by the largest of the multinational corporations in order to bring about a new world order.[158]

Plato's *Republic* is the source book of all dictatorships. Plato's blueprint for a new society begins with breaking up the existing social structure by whatever means necessary, including force, in order to establish the "ideal" society. There would be three classes: the special ruling class, a powerful army and the working class. There would be slaves also, but slaves would not be considered citizens. Marriage would be eliminated. Women would be equal with men—equal to fight wars with men and perform labor like men. Sexual activity would be controlled and limited by the State. There would be selective breeding of children and children considered inferior or crippled would be destroyed. People would be induced to believe falsehoods taught as religious principles. Myths would convey important "truths" to young or untrained minds. Religious institutions would be regulated by a recognized national authority. Priests would have no authority over beliefs, but would be officials whose duty it would be to perform rituals. War would cease when all states are united in a world-state according to the principles prescribed by Plato. And Plato was prepared to place the control of the State in the hands of a single man.[159]

COMMENTARY: Each nation has its "ruling elite," a wealthy aristocracy that comprises its ruling class. Historically, government has been the servant of private wealth. Political and economic power is concentrated in the hands of this ruling elite that is the hidden power behind government. They control the big banks, large corporations, major communications media, influential foundations; in fact, their power encompasses all areas of society. Though they fight amongst themselves for control, these ruling class families have formed an alliance amongst themselves for world domination. This is the real meaning of "GLOBALISM," which is costing Americans their jobs as work is outsourced to foreign countries for increased profits and in order to weaken the infrastructure of America and reduce its standard of living to facilitate its incorporation into the New World Order being engineered by this hierarchy of wealthy families. Their greatest tool and weapon is money. . . and the ignorance of the public.

A SPECIAL NOTE ABOUT WAR:

"All warfare is based on deception," wrote Chinese General Sun Tsu in "The Art of War" more than twenty-five hundred years ago. He goes on to say that *"supreme excellence consists in breaking the enemy's resistance without fighting."* Inducing stress, anxiety, fear and terror in a population is a strategy of psychological warfare. Thinking and behavior can be altered when people are subjected to intense and prolonged stress.

"In states of human fear and excitement the most wildly improbable suggestions can be accepted by apparently sensible people," wrote British psychiatrist Dr. William Sargant in his 1957 book "Battle for the Mind," which examines the psychology of religious conversion and political brainwashing. He concludes: *"The politico-religious struggle for the mind of man may well be won by whoever becomes most conversant with the normal and abnormal functions of the brain, and is readiest to make use of the knowledge gained."*

"War is a racket," wrote Marine Major General Smedley Butler in 1935 in his book by that same title. This two-time recipient of the Congressional Medal of Honor goes on to say: *"A racket is best described, I believe, as something that is not what it seems to the majority of people. Only a small 'inside' group knows what it is about. It is conducted for the benefit of the very few, at the expense of the very many."* The United States is not a democracy. It is not a republic, though this is what the Founders intended. It is a plutocracy, government by the wealthy, run by a small ruling class elite.

SECTION 13

Education as Propaganda

All totalitarian movements are vitally concerned with the indoctrination of the young. Both Mussolini and Hitler organized youth before their rise to power.[160] Because of this, popular culture (movies, TV and music) is of great importance as is a general State education. Plato advised censorship of literature for schools and advocated control of poetry, music, painting, sculpture and architecture.[161] Dr. W. J. Spillman, former chief of the Federal Farm Management Bureau of the Department of Agriculture, stated in a letter to the *New York Globe* of March 28, 1919: "Nine years ago I was approached by an agent of Mr. Rockefeller with the statement that his object in establishing the General Education Board was to gain control of the educational institutions of the country so that all men employed in them might be 'right'."[162]

The General Education Board was organized in 1902 by John D. Rockefeller, founder of the Standard Oil Company.[163] The General Education Board was the first of the Rockefeller foundations and influenced the development of America's educational system.[164] The objective was stated by Rockefeller and Baptist minister Rev. Frederick Taylor Gates, the guiding force in many of Rockefeller's enterprises, in the first publication of the General Education Board, the "Occasional Paper No. 1," in 1904: "In our dreams we have limitless resources and the people yield themselves with perfect docility to our molding hands. The present educational conventions fade from our minds, and unhampered by tradition, we work our own good will upon a grateful and responsive rural folk. We shall not try to make these people or any of their children into philosophers or men of learning, or of science... The task we set before ourselves is very simple as well as a very beautiful one, to train these people as we find them to a perfectly ideal life just where they are. So we will organize our children into a community and teach them to do in a perfect way the things their fathers and mothers are doing in an imperfect way, in the homes, in the shop and on the farm."[165]

Education of the young is used to condition them to what comes later, thereby eliminating the difference between propaganda and education.[166] Propaganda cannot work effectively without education. The mind is conditioned with vast amounts of information posing as "facts" and "knowledge" dispensed for ulterior motives.[167] Remember the first principle behind mental programming: distraction. With propaganda, distraction focuses attention on information that is false. Repetition of the false information imbeds it in your subconscious mind so that your acceptance of its truth and accuracy becomes a conditioned response, circumventing analysis. Therefore, you accept this information as true without thinking about it. This is especially true in school where there is pressure to accept what is presented as true because that is what is expected of you. Remember that your trust in the source of information determines whether or not you accept it. What people think can be controlled by controlling information. **People can be led to believe something that is not true when that information is presented by an accepted authority and repeated over and over again until its acceptance becomes a conditioned response.**

COMMENTARY: There could be no effective propaganda without education. In the early 1900's there began a dramatic shift in emphasis in American education from *intellectual* development to *socialization.* The goals of education became political and social rather than academic. This was due in large part to John Dewey who denied the existence of God and moral absolutes and we are experiencing the disastrous effect it has had in destabilizing society. Professor Dewey based his educational reforms on the experimental psychology developed at Leipzig University by Wilhelm Wundt. Professor Wundt believed that Man had no spirit. In his view, Man was only a stimulus response animal. This kind of thinking led to the principles of conditioning developed by Ivan Pavlov and behavioral psychologists John Watson and B.F. Skinner. As a result, schools became indoctrination centers designed to bring about a *new social order.*

MIND CONTROL IS BEING USED ON AN UNSUSPECTING PUBLIC. MIND CONTROL IS BEING USED ON AN UNSUSPECTING PUBLIC.
MIND CONTROL IS BEING USED ON AN UNSUSPECTING PUBLIC. MIND CONTROL IS BEING USED ON AN UNSUSPECTING PUBLIC.
MIND CONTROL IS BEING USED ON AN UNSUSPECTING PUBLIC. MIND CONTROL IS BEING USED ON AN UNSUSPECTING PUBLIC.
MIND CONTROL IS BEING USED ON AN UNSUSPECTING PUBLIC. MIND CONTROL IS BEING USED ON AN UNSUSPECTING PUBLIC.
MIND CONTROL IS BEING USED ON AN UNSUSPECTING PUBLIC. MIND CONTROL IS BEING USED ON AN UNSUSPECTING PUBLIC.
MIND CONTROL IS BEING USED ON AN UNSUSPECTING PUBLIC. MIND CONTROL IS BEING USED ON AN UNSUSPECTING PUBLIC.
MIND CONTROL IS BEING USED ON AN UNSUSPECTING PUBLIC. MIND CONTROL IS BEING USED ON AN UNSUSPECTING PUBLIC.
MIND CONTROL IS BEING USED ON AN UNSUSPECTING PUBLIC. MIND CONTROL IS BEING USED ON AN UNSUSPECTING PUBLIC.
MIND CONTROL IS BEING USED ON AN UNSUSPECTING PUBLIC. MIND CONTROL IS BEING USED ON AN UNSUSPECTING PUBLIC.
MIND CONTROL IS BEING USED ON AN UNSUSPECTING PUBLIC. MIND CONTROL IS BEING USED ON AN UNSUSPECTING PUBLIC.
MIND CONTROL IS BEING USED ON AN UNSUSPECTING PUBLIC. MIND CONTROL IS BEING USED ON AN UNSUSPECTING PUBLIC.
MIND CONTROL IS BEING USED ON AN UNSUSPECTING PUBLIC. MIND CONTROL IS BEING USED ON AN UNSUSPECTING PUBLIC.
MIND CONTROL IS BEING USED ON AN UNSUSPECTING PUBLIC. MIND CONTROL IS BEING USED ON AN UNSUSPECTING PUBLIC.
MIND CONTROL IS BEING USED ON AN UNSUSPECTING PUBLIC. MIND CONTROL IS BEING USED ON AN UNSUSPECTING PUBLIC.
MIND CONTROL IS BEING USED ON AN UNSUSPECTING PUBLIC. MIND CONTROL IS BEING USED ON AN UNSUSPECTING PUBLIC.
MIND CONTROL IS BEING USED ON AN UNSUSPECTING PUBLIC. MIND CONTROL IS BEING USED ON AN UNSUSPECTING PUBLIC.
MIND CONTROL IS BEING USED ON AN UNSUSPECTING PUBLIC. MIND CONTROL IS BEING USED ON AN UNSUSPECTING PUBLIC.

SECTION 14
Communism

For years the message has been repeated over and over again that Communism is the enemy, that Communism seeks to conquer the world. This is a distraction to draw attention away from what has actually been happening. It is true that Communism seeks world domination, but this is not the whole story. Since 1917 the Soviet Union openly and consistently advocated the overthrow of Western governments. However, Soviet economic development was largely the result of Western technology from Western companies. This transfer of technology was allowed and encouraged by Western governments, primarily the United States, Great Britain, Germany, France and Italy.[168] "The penetration of early Soviet industry by Western companies and individuals was remarkable," writes Antony C. Sutton in the three-volume history *Western Technology and Soviet Economic Development.* [169] In June 1944, W. Averell Harriman, U.S. ambassador to the Soviet Union, reported to the State Department: "Stalin paid tribute to the assistance rendered by the United States to Soviet industry before and during the war. He said that about two-thirds of all large industrial enterprises in the Soviet Union had been built with United States help or technical assistance."[170] The Soviets received Western technologies with military applications from 1917 to the present.[171] The major conclusion presented by Sutton in his research study is that "Western technology has been, and continues to be, the most important factor in Soviet economic development."[172] Soviet dependence on the West escaped public attention primarily because of propaganda. Censorship and travel restrictions within the Soviet Union were designed to hide the massive technological transfers from the West as the primary explanation for Soviet economic and military growth. The Soviet Union was a Frankenstein monster that was created by the West.

The first edition of *The Communist Manifesto* was published in London in 1848. The first plank calls for the abolition of all private property. Owning your own home has become an eroding dream for many Americans. As interest rates rise, home sales decline. The percentage of Americans owning homes has fallen since 1980.[173] Home and farm foreclosures are a clear danger to growing numbers of Americans.[174] Family farms are rapidly becoming a thing of the past. More and more farmers are taking jobs off the farm, as the ownership of the means of production become more and more concentrated in industrialized "superfarms."[175] The second plank advocates a graduated or progressive income tax. On October 3, 1913, Congress enacted the first income tax under the sixteenth amendment to the Constitution, thus instituting the graduated income tax proposed by Karl Marx.[176] Earlier attempts to impose the graduated income tax were declared unconstitutional by the Supreme Court. In 1902 the Chief Justice stated: "It is a method to enslave our people, and deprive them of their liberty and right to the fruit of their labors."[177] The graduated income tax was designed to squeeze the middle class out of existence.[178] The fifth plank of *The Communist Manifesto*: "Centralization of credit in the hands of the State, by means of a national bank with State capital and an exclusive monopoly." On December 22, 1913 the Federal Reserve Act was passed. "When the President signs this act, the invisible government by the money power will be legalized," Congressman Charles A. Lindbergh, Sr. told Congress after the vote. The members of the Federal Reserve Board are appointed by the President for fourteen-year terms. The Federal Reserve controls the nation's money supply and interest rates, and thereby manipulates the entire economy, creating inflation or deflation, recession or boom, sending the stock market up or down at whim. "From now on depressions will be scientifically created," commented Congressman Lindbergh. Congressman Louis McFadden, Chairman of the House Banking and Currency Committee, commented that the Crash of '29 was not an accident. It was a carefully engineered event. "The international bankers sought to bring about a condition of despair here so that they might emerge as the rulers of us all."[179] It is significant to note that all banking in the Soviet Union was not declared a State monopoly until December 14, 1917.[180] The sixth plank calls for the centralization of the means of communication in the hands of the State. Even though the government controls all the means of communication in a dictatorship, the government doesn't necessarily have to own all the means of communication.[181] A concentration of ownership in the mass communications industry exists in the United States.[182] Without mass media, there could be no effective propaganda. To make the co-ordination of propaganda possible, the media must be concentrated, the number of news agencies reduced, and press, publishing, radio, television and film monopolies established. Only through concentration in a few hands of a large number of media can there be an orchestration and continuity to propaganda and the application of scientific methods to influence public attitudes and behavior.[183]

The number of unmarried couples living together has more than tripled since 1970. More and more young adults are living with their parents.[184] The number of divorces in 1979 was nearly triple the number reported twenty years earlier.[185] For the first time in American history, white men are a minority in the nation's work force and the number of working women is steadily increasing.[186] *The Communist Manifesto* advocates the abolition of the family. Plato's blueprint for establishing the "ideal" State begins with breaking up the existing social order. This is being accomplished scientifically through the manipulation of the economy and the communications media. Movies, TV, and music are of great importance in molding young and untrained minds. In *1984*, George Orwell predicted that the State would seek to control the sex drive, specifically by using psychological techniques to eliminate orgasm.[187] The rock video *Relax* by Frankie Goes to Hollywood, with pulsating light patterns as a visual distraction, presents a verbal program: "Relax. Don't do it, when you want to go to it. Relax. Don't do it, when you want to come." The lyrics are repeated over and over again to the pulsating beat of the music. Any repeating light or sound pattern can lead you into the hypnotic state of mind where you are the most receptive to mental programming. Many rock videos, TV programs and movies mix violence with sex. The *Friday the 13th* series of films about a maniac who chops up teenagers at a summer camp, shows young people, especially the women, being punished for having sex.[188] J. R. from *Dallas* and Alexis from *Dynasty* treat sex in the same way they treat business, as a way to satisfy themselves and get the better of someone else. Television, movies and music strongly shape the social attitudes of young people and breed disappointment in interpersonal relationships, encourage antagonism, suspicion and sometimes contempt between the sexes.[189] All of this is meant to facilitate the elimination of the family as proposed by Karl Marx and Plato in order to control people under a dictatorship.

In *1984*, personal relationships are replaced by political activism and devotion to the State.[190]

A report released in 1982 by the National Institute of Mental Health said "violence on television does lead to aggressive behavior by children and teenagers who watch the programs." According to the 1982 Nielson Report on Television, the typical high school graduate has witnessed about 150,000 violent acts on television, including an estimated 25,000 deaths.[191] Dr. Thomas Narut from the U.S. Naval Hospital at NATO headquarters in Naples has investigated the use of film to train servicemen who were not inclined to kill to be able to do so. Films were screened which showed people being maimed or killed violently to desensitize the men to such acts.[192] A progressively more graphic depiction of violence on television and in the movies desensitizes the viewer, especially young people, to real-life violence, and at the same time older people, becoming fearful, demand that something be done. Note that this is the same strategy used in the campaign against marijuana. Marijuana use is encouraged among young people, as in the Cheech and Chong movies, while older people are scared into demanding tougher legislation and penalties. Government propaganda directs public opinion to demand what the government has already decided to do. Movies, TV, and music often present violence as acceptable and sometimes laudable behavior. And older people are scared into demanding tougher legislation and penalties because of this very same behavior, bringing the country closer and closer to a police state legislated by law.

A University of Massachusetts study of crime programs on television reveals that law enforcement officers routinely break-and-enter illegally, fail to inform suspects of their rights, terrorize and coerce witnesses and commit bribery. Constitutional guarantees are regarded as bothersome "technicalities" that hinder the police in the performance of their duty. These programs erode public support for protections granted under the Bill of Rights. Professors Katsch and Arons, who conducted the study, say: "Police shows seem to reduce the ordinary citizens' awareness of constitutional rights and responsibilities. Many people engrossed in the drama of rapid-fire action or preoccupied with violence fail even to notice blatant police-state tactics."[193] Metro-Dade County Police Lt. Pete Cuccarro quit as technical advisor of the TV detective series *Miami Vice*. In the second episode, a homicide detective roughs up a suspect and two undercover officers allow an informant to use drugs in their presence. "To subliminally suggest that those things are OK is not acceptable," said Cuccarro.[194] Crime programs on television have the political effect of "softening up" public opinion.[195] Government propaganda directs public opinion to demand or at least docilely accept what the government has already decided to do. During its 1983-84 term, the Supreme Court significantly expanded police powers and governmental authority while curtailing individual rights, thus enacting into law principles much like those presented on TV crime shows.[196]

Thomas Jefferson believed that government governs best which governs least. The Founding Fathers considered that the primary purpose of government is to promote the happiness of society. The Framers of the Constitution adopted two basic guidelines to achieve society's happiness, safety, liberty and justice: First, power must not be allowed to concentrate either in individuals or institutions. Second, the ultimate power must reside with the people. All lawful government is founded on the consent of the people.[197] "One of the irreversible currents I have noted in thirty-four years of reporting is the hankering of our leaders to transform themselves from servants into sovereigns," writes columnist Jack Anderson.[198] James Madison said: "The accumulation of all powers, legislative, executive and judicial in the same hands, whether of one, a few, or many, and whether hereditary, self-appointed, or elective, may justly be pronounced the very definition of tyranny."[199] Recognizing that the primary threat to society was arbitrary, unrestrained, unaccountable power, the Framers of the Constitution sought to restrain government so that it could not restrain the liberties and rights of the people. Their device for this end was the separation of powers so that no segment of government could amass enough power to establish a dictatorship. However, the sovereignty of the people has disintegrated because the separation of powers has broken down.[200] Power has been steadily centralized in the executive branch of the federal government.[201]

COMMENTARY: Norman Dodd, research director for the Special Committee to Investigate Tax Exempt Foundations created by the 83rd Congress, was invited in November 1953 to meet in New York with Rowan Gaither, president of the Ford Foundation. Mr. Gaither made a most revealing admission: "... *Mr. Dodd, we operate here under directives which emanate from the White House. . . The substance of the directives under which we operate is that we shall use our grant-making power to alter life in the United States so that we can be comfortably merged with the Soviet Union.*"

While the Communist world is becoming more like the West, America is going in the opposite direction. The political concepts of the United States have undergone a gradual alteration in order to promote "administrative government" by appointed bureaucrats rather than the constitutionally mandated representative government by elected officials. A network of organizations headquartered at what is called *"1313"* at the University of Chicago have been working to restructure local, state and federal government. *1313* affiliates developed the regional framework to merge city-county government, then county-district, district-state, state-region, and on to a region-international merger into a one-world government. The program of these social science organizations is a *totally managed and controlled society.*

Centralization of government functions is a basic socialist principle. Centralization takes government away from the people. The key factor is control. The computer-based "Planning, Programming and Budgeting System" is the mechanism for that control. This system was promoted as a modern space-age method for budgeting and accounting, but it is used to achieve behavioral objectives designed to capture the decision-making process of government. Systematic management and control of society replaces self-government.

A one-world government means the loss of national sovereignty for the United States. All areas of our culture have been corrupted in order to promote this program and psychological warfare is being waged against the public to accept it, and even demand some of the changes necessary to bring about a New Dark Age on this planet.

The plan is as old as history with its modern manifestation having reared its ugly head in 1776 when Adam Weishaupt, Professor of Canon Law at the

University of Ingolstadt in Bavaria, founded the Order of the Illuminati ("the Enlightened Ones"). The goal of the Illuminati was the creation of a **New World Order.** This was to be accomplished by infiltrating all areas of society and destroying civilization from within. A nation with high ethical and moral standards is difficult if not impossible to conquer. A degraded nation has no defense against conquest.

"A nation can survive its fools, and even the ambitious. But it cannot survive treason from within. An enemy at the gates is less formidable, for he is known and carries his banners openly. But the traitor moves among those within the gates freely, his sly whispers rustling through all the alleys, heard in the very halls of government itself. For the traitor appears not a traitor; he speaks in accents familiar to his victims, and he wears their face and their garments, and he appeals to the baseness that lies deep in the hearts of all men. He rots the soul of a nation. He works secretly and unknown in the night to undermine the pillars of a city; he infects the body politic so that it can longer resist. A murderer is less to be feared."

- Marcus Tullius Cicero, 42 B.C.

A Speech in the Roman Senate

"We are on the verge of a global transformation. All we need is the right major crisis and the nations will accept the New World Order."

-David Rockefeller

speaking at a UN Business Conference, Sept. 14, 1994

MIND CONTROL IS BEING USED ON AN UNSUSPECTING PUBLIC. MIND CONTROL IS BEING USED ON AN UNSUSPECTING PUBLIC.
MIND CONTROL IS BEING USED ON AN UNSUSPECTING PUBLIC. MIND CONTROL IS BEING USED ON AN UNSUSPECTING PUBLIC.
MIND CONTROL IS BEING USED ON AN UNSUSPECTING PUBLIC. MIND CONTROL IS BEING USED ON AN UNSUSPECTING PUBLIC.
MIND CONTROL IS BEING USED ON AN UNSUSPECTING PUBLIC. MIND CONTROL IS BEING USED ON AN UNSUSPECTING PUBLIC.
MIND CONTROL IS BEING USED ON AN UNSUSPECTING PUBLIC. MIND CONTROL IS BEING USED ON AN UNSUSPECTING PUBLIC.
MIND CONTROL IS BEING USED ON AN UNSUSPECTING PUBLIC. MIND CONTROL IS BEING USED ON AN UNSUSPECTING PUBLIC.
MIND CONTROL IS BEING USED ON AN UNSUSPECTING PUBLIC. MIND CONTROL IS BEING USED ON AN UNSUSPECTING PUBLIC.
MIND CONTROL IS BEING USED ON AN UNSUSPECTING PUBLIC. MIND CONTROL IS BEING USED ON AN UNSUSPECTING PUBLIC.
MIND CONTROL IS BEING USED ON AN UNSUSPECTING PUBLIC. MIND CONTROL IS BEING USED ON AN UNSUSPECTING PUBLIC.
MIND CONTROL IS BEING USED ON AN UNSUSPECTING PUBLIC. MIND CONTROL IS BEING USED ON AN UNSUSPECTING PUBLIC.
MIND CONTROL IS BEING USED ON AN UNSUSPECTING PUBLIC. MIND CONTROL IS BEING USED ON AN UNSUSPECTING PUBLIC.
MIND CONTROL IS BEING USED ON AN UNSUSPECTING PUBLIC. MIND CONTROL IS BEING USED ON AN UNSUSPECTING PUBLIC.
MIND CONTROL IS BEING USED ON AN UNSUSPECTING PUBLIC. MIND CONTROL IS BEING USED ON AN UNSUSPECTING PUBLIC.
MIND CONTROL IS BEING USED ON AN UNSUSPECTING PUBLIC. MIND CONTROL IS BEING USED ON AN UNSUSPECTING PUBLIC.
MIND CONTROL IS BEING USED ON AN UNSUSPECTING PUBLIC. MIND CONTROL IS BEING USED ON AN UNSUSPECTING PUBLIC.
MIND CONTROL IS BEING USED ON AN UNSUSPECTING PUBLIC. MIND CONTROL IS BEING USED ON AN UNSUSPECTING PUBLIC.
MIND CONTROL IS BEING USED ON AN UNSUSPECTING PUBLIC. MIND CONTROL IS BEING USED ON AN UNSUSPECTING PUBLIC.
MIND CONTROL IS BEING USED ON AN UNSUSPECTING PUBLIC. MIND CONTROL IS BEING USED ON AN UNSUSPECTING PUBLIC.

SECTION 15

The Bible and

Fundamentalism

President Reagan signed a proclamation making 1983 the Year of the Bible. Speaking at the annual convention of the National Religious Broadcasters January 31, 1983, he stated that "Within the covers of that single Book are all the answers to all the problems that face us today, if we'd only look there."[202] Holding up a Bible, Rev. Jerry Falwell admonishes: "If a man stands by this book, vote for him. If he doesn't, don't."[203] Politics and religion are intertwined in the United States. The Bible has exerted an unrivaled influence on American culture, politics and social life. There was a time when Bible study was the core of public education. Americans publish more Bibles than any other people. Only in America is there a "Bible belt" with Bible camps, Bible colleges, Bible institutes and Bible bookstores. Our nation's battles have been religious crusades as preachers and politicians used the Bible to justify their causes. The history of the Bible in America is a history of conflicting interpretations. Both slave-owners and abolitionists cited the Bible for their cause, as did civil-rights marchers and segregationists in the 1960s.[204]

"The entire Bible from Genesis to Revelation is the inerrant word of God, and totally accurate in all respects," says Jerry Falwell.[205] Fundamentalists believe the Bible to be the ultimate authority in all matters, the "revealed, inspired, infallible and inerrant Word of God."[206] They spread the Word in accordance with the New Testament commandment: "Go ye into all the world and preach the gospel to every creature."[207] Religious programming on TV is flooding the airways.[208] One of the biggest forces in religious broadcasting is the Christian Broadcasting Network. It is the largest noncommercial broadcasting network in the world. *The 700 Club*, hosted by CBN founder Pat Robertson, is seen around the world.[209] *The PTL*

Club, hosted by Jim Bakker, was a talk show in a format similar to Johnny Carson's *Tonight Show.* There was Jerry Falwell's *Old-Time Gospel Hour,* Jimmy Swaggart, James Robison, Kenneth Copeland and old-timers Oral Roberts, Billy Graham and Rex Humbard. The newest entry is the American Christian Television System of the Southern Baptist Convention.

TV evangelist Jimmy Swaggart has said: "Your mind is the gateway to your spirit. The mind is the place where the battleground is."[210] The fundamentalist movement demonstrates mastery of propaganda and mind control over its adherents and converts. Because of its sense of mission, the fundamentalist movement resembles past totalitarian movements by transforming political, economic and social issues into a Crusade. Its machinery for control consists of a highly-organized and well-funded political machine, a vast mass-communications network, an independent (Christian) education system, Bible studies, churches and missionary organizations. "They believe that they possess the ultimate truth which has been revealed through the Bible and that their interpretation of Scriptures constitutes the irrefutable will of God," said former Senator Frank Church of Idaho.[211] "We must be obedient to the Word of God," says Jerry Falwell. "Whatsoever He sayeth unto you, do! That's all there is to it!"[212] Repetition of verses from the Bible is a predominant part of the fundamentalist program and all thoughts, feelings and actions are checked against it. As a result, all actions of the "believers" can be controlled and directed with scientific precision because of their obedience to an unquestioned mental program prescribing the limits for all human behavior.[213]

COMMENTARY: Scriptures are a road map to God Consciousness. To worship the road map does not get one to the destination. A literal interpretation of what is presented symbolically makes the symbol more important than what it was meant to represent. Words are symbols that represent reality. But the words are not the reality themselves. That is known through insight and understanding. In fact, true knowledge is received as a revelation from within and is not the product of thought.

Jesus (Yeshua) was highly critical of the religious authorities of his day, the Pharisees, for "teaching as doctrines the commandments of men". The Talmud is the oral tradition of Judaism in written form. Throughout history whenever its contents have become known to "outsiders," it has been a source of contention and conflict with other religions. It is especially anti-Christian, maniacal in its hatred for Jesus Christ and obsessive in its compulsion for control and domination of other people.

Phariseeism and Christianity are not compatible. And yet the teachings of the Pharisees have infiltrated Christianity and other religions. The Jewish people were under the control of the Pharisees during the time of Jesus as much as they are today. Judaism traces its descent to the Pharisees. Judaism is Phariseeism. It is not the religion of the ancient Hebrews of the Old Testament. Phariseeism is the Spirit and Consciousness of Materialism.

Deuteronomy is the basis for Old Testament Law and the political program for world domination. It was the Levitical priesthood that promoted the "Chosen People" idea telling their followers that if they obeyed the Law, they would inherit the promised land and dominion over all peoples. The rewards were exclusively material. The priestly doctrine was to kill and enslave the heathen, steal his property and women. The call to massacre abounds in the Old Testament. A scorched-earth policy was the rule. The purpose of existence under the "Law" was the destruction and enslavement of others for wealth and power. The faithful were admonished to destroy other religions and if a "prophet" or "dreamer of dreams" should arise to turn them from their ways, he should be put to death. It was the priesthood that put the commandments and judgments of God in writing. And so they put it down as it pleased THEM, and thus organized a group separate unto themselves to be used as a disruptive force among nations. The God of the New Testament says "love your neighbor as yourself," while the God of Deuteronomy says to "utterly destroy your neighbor." When combining the Old Testament and the New Testament, there is a message of hate and a message of love that makes one schizophrenic and double-minded if one tries to adhere to both. *"Beware ye of the leaven of the Pharisees, which is hypocrisy."* (Luke 12:1)

World Evangelism, under the guise of Christianity, is promoting the world government dream of the Pharisees. The false teaching of apostate Christianity is that the kingdom of God on earth is in the future under Jesus Christ as a political leader. The message that Christ is going to return to establish an earthly kingdom is not consistent with the teachings of Christ who said: "My kingdom is not of this world." (John 18:36) The kingdom of God is spiritual, not material. Belief in a future earthly world political order that is Christian is Phariseeism under a different name.

Teaching Phariseeism as Christianity is an attempt to program and condition the population to accept and even demand a political leader as a messiah in the name of Christ. During the time of Jesus, the Jewish people, under the propaganda of the Pharisees, expected a political messiah to deliver them from Rome. Today, many Christians are expecting a political leader to deliver America and the world from Satan. Jesus never instructed his disciples to take over the world in a material and political sense. There is nothing in the Bible about taking over Rome for Jesus. The message of national salvation is the same propaganda promoted by the Nazis and National Socialism. Salvation is individual, not national; and spiritual, not material.

Dominion-theology, a part of the deception, is a pretext for political dominion, using religion for ends that are contrary to the purpose of religion: spiritual emancipation from material consciousness. Dominion-theology is the belief that Old Testament Law should be established and enforced in America and throughout the world. The proponents of this belief consider it their moral duty to act as agents of God's wrath in administering punishment. Instituting Old Testament restitution would mean that offenders would have to pay back victims, including the State, in money or in labor as a slave. The death penalty for capital crimes in the Old Testament includes adultery, fornication, blasphemy, apostasy, idolatry and striking or cursing a parent in addition to murder, kidnapping and rape. Stoning is part of Old Testament Law and so is death by decapitation in accordance with the Noahide Laws. Those who have been indoctrinated into dominion-theology believe it to be a moral obligation for Christians to take back every institution in society in the name of Jesus. The Bible and the Bible alone is to govern all thinking. And there is no tolerance for the heathen religions, that is any religion other than their own. They believe that Christianity is destined to take over all the kingdoms of the earth and that Christians have a holy mandate to reclaim America and the world for Christ. The goal of dominion-theology is world conquest – the agenda of the Pharisees. Unnoticed by most is the fact that a significant segment of the population is being propagandized into a revolutionary movement for the takeover of America and the world. "The Great Commission" of the 28th chapter of Matthew, verses 18 to 21, where Christ commands his disciples to teach and make disciples of all nations has absolutely nothing to do with the political and material conquest of the world. On the contrary, the only conquest that is meaningful spiritually is the conquest of one's own self by the purification of one's materially contaminated consciousness. It is only by teaching that kind of conquest that one fulfills the call of "The Great Commission".

MIND CONTROL IS BEING USED ON AN UNSUSPECTING PUBLIC. MIND CONTROL IS BEING USED ON AN UNSUSPECTING PUBLIC.
MIND CONTROL IS BEING USED ON AN UNSUSPECTING PUBLIC. MIND CONTROL IS BEING USED ON AN UNSUSPECTING PUBLIC.
MIND CONTROL IS BEING USED ON AN UNSUSPECTING PUBLIC. MIND CONTROL IS BEING USED ON AN UNSUSPECTING PUBLIC.
MIND CONTROL IS BEING USED ON AN UNSUSPECTING PUBLIC. MIND CONTROL IS BEING USED ON AN UNSUSPECTING PUBLIC.
MIND CONTROL IS BEING USED ON AN UNSUSPECTING PUBLIC. MIND CONTROL IS BEING USED ON AN UNSUSPECTING PUBLIC.
MIND CONTROL IS BEING USED ON AN UNS   BEING USED ON AN UNSUSPECTING PUBLIC.
MIND CONTROL IS BEING USED ON AN   BEING USED ON AN UNSUSPECTING PUBLIC.

SECTION 16
Occult (Secret) Knowledge

MIND CONT   TING PUBLIC.
MIND CON   TING PUBLIC.
MIND CON   TING PUBLIC.
MIND CONTROL IS BEING USED ON AN UNSUSPECTING PUBLIC. MIND CONTROL IS BEING USED ON AN UNSUSPECTING PUBLIC.
MIND CONTROL IS BEING USED ON AN UNSUSPECTING PUBLIC. MIND CONTROL IS BEING USED ON AN UNSUSPECTING PUBLIC.
MIND CONTROL IS BEING USED ON AN UNSUSPECTING PUBLIC. MIND CONTROL IS BEING USED ON AN UNSUSPECTING PUBLIC.
MIND CONTROL IS BEING USED ON AN UNSUSPECTING PUBLIC. MIND CONTROL IS BEING USED ON AN UNSUSPECTING PUBLIC.
MIND CONTROL IS BEING USED ON AN UNSUSPECTING PUBLIC. MIND CONTROL IS BEING USED ON AN UNSUSPECTING PUBLIC.

Both the Old Testament and New Testament severely prohibit any examination and exploration of the occult.[214] Remember, secret knowledge is the basis of all power. Ancient religious cults reserved part of their teachings for disclosure to a select few who were taught certain secret doctrines. Those initiated in the "mysteries" were committed to strict secrecy.[215] Ancient Egyptian mysteries were a key to complete knowledge. This knowledge was preserved in the "Hermetic" writings of the legendary Egyptian prophet Hermes Trismegistus describing the soul's journey upward through higher spheres. The Cabala, a Hebrew mysticism that evolved in France and Spain in the 12th and 13th centuries, conceives God as infinite Light from which Creation emanates through ten successive spheres called Sepiroth. Though man separated himself from Sepiroth long ago, their divine attributes remain active in him, and he may, through them, return to the source of Light.[216] The Hermetic-Cabalist view of life is the belief in man's power to tap the natural forces from higher spheres.[217] This is "the Force" in *Star Wars*. What was fundamental to all the mysteries, without exception, was the revelation of the true meaning of death.[218]

"And as it is appointed unto men once to die, but after this the judgment," states Hebrews 9:27. The significance of this teaching is the absolute denial of the doctrine of karma where your deeds have an inescapable influence on your destiny, where numerous cycles of birth and death are necessary as a program of experience and learning in the upward journey to spiritual perfection and graduation from this particular plane of existence. Reincarnation was once a part of Biblical teaching, but was censored. The New Testament was not recorded until long after Jesus died.[219] Christianity became the *official*

63

religion of the Roman Empire in the third century.[220] A number of differing gospels existed at the time of the Council of Nicea in A.D. 325 where the present Bible was decided upon. Those judged unacceptable were destroyed, only what was considered acceptable remained.[221] Any changes, deletions, additions made by Church councils or by the monarch King James would have a profound effect on the masses for the Bible could be used either to control or liberate them.[222] In its campaign against heresy, the Church destroyed most of the ancient literature by burning libraries.[223] What people think can be controlled by controlling information.

COMMENTARY: The Cabala is the source book on magic in the tradition of ancient Babylon. It is concerned with manipulating the energy of Universal Consciousness through incantation, mind action, amulets and natural plant drugs. It is a lexicon of sorcery, the casting of spells and summoning of spirits to do one's bidding. The existence of evil spirits is mentioned throughout the Bible. Various diseases and ailments were attributed to evil spirits. Yeshua (Jesus) and his disciples cast out evil spirits, cured blindness, leprosy and fever. They possessed secret knowledge. The most comprehensive prohibition against seeking knowledge of forbidden topics appears in the 18th chapter of Deuteronomy, verses 10 to 12, prohibiting divination, hypnotism, magic and necromancy (communicating with the dead, i.e., spirits) knowledge the priesthood jealously guarded for itself.

Jesus taught a secret doctrine to his disciples: *"Unto you it is given to know the mystery of the kingdom of God; but unto those who are without, all these things are done in parables."* (Mark 4:11) In many religions there are two teachings: the outer teaching for the masses and the inner or secret teaching for the disciples and initiates.

"I received from the messenger of God two kinds of knowledge," said Mohammed. *"One of these I taught. . . if I had taught them the other, it would have broken their throats."* Buddha said: *"O disciples, the things which I have discovered and have not told you are more numerous than those which I have told you."* And Jesus said: *"I have yet many things to say unto you, but ye cannot bear them now."* (John 6:12) In other words, there is more to be revealed. Information is given according to time, place, circumstances and the consciousness of those receiving the information.

MIND CONTROL IS BEING USED ON AN UNSUSPECTING PUBLIC. MIND CONTROL IS BEING USED ON AN UNSUSPECTING PUBLIC.
MIND CONTROL IS BEING USED ON AN UNSUSPECTING PUBLIC. MIND CONTROL IS BEING USED ON AN UNSUSPECTING PUBLIC.
MIND CONTROL IS BEING USED ON AN UNSUSPECTING PUBLIC. MIND CONTROL IS BEING USED ON AN UNSUSPECTING PUBLIC.
MIND CONTROL IS BEING USED ON AN UNS   BEING USED ON AN UNSUSPECTING PUBLIC.
MIND CONTROL IS BEING USED ON AN UNS   BEING USED ON AN UNSUSPECTING PUBLIC.
MIND CONTROL IS BEING USED ON AN UNS   BEING USED ON AN UNSUSPECTING PUBLIC.
MIND CONTROL IS BEING USED ON AN UNS   BEING USED ON AN UNSUSPECTING PUBLIC.
MIND CONTROL IS BEING USED ON AN UNSUSPECTING PUBLIC. MIND CONTROL IS BEING USED ON AN UNSUSPECTING PUBLIC.
MIND CONTROL IS BEING USED ON AN UNSUSPECTING PUBLIC. MIND CONTROL IS BEING USED ON AN UNSUSPECTING PUBLIC.
MIND CONTROL IS BEING USED   ON AN UNSUSPECTING PUBLIC.
MIND CONTROL IS BEING USED   ON AN UNSUSPECTING PUBLIC.
MIND CONTROL IS BEING USED   ON AN UNSUSPECTING PUBLIC.
MIND CONTROL IS BEING USED ON AN UNSUSPECTING PUBLIC. MIND CONTROL IS BEING USED ON AN UNSUSPECTING PUBLIC.
MIND CONTROL IS BEING USED ON AN UNSUSPECTING PUBLIC. MIND CONTROL IS BEING USED ON AN UNSUSPECTING PUBLIC.
MIND CONTROL IS BEING USED ON AN UNSUSPECTING PUBLIC. MIND CONTROL IS BEING USED ON AN UNSUSPECTING PUBLIC.
MIND CONTROL IS BEING USED ON AN UNSUSPECTING PUBLIC. MIND CONTROL IS BEING USED ON AN UNSUSPECTING PUBLIC.
MIND CONTROL IS BEING USED ON AN UNSUSPECTING PUBLIC. MIND CONTROL IS BEING USED ON AN UNSUSPECTING PUBLIC.
MIND CONTROL IS BEING USED ON AN UNSUSPECTING PUBLIC. MIND CONTROL IS BEING USED ON AN UNSUSPECTING PUBLIC.

SECTION 17
Parapsychology

Historically, parapsychology emerged from nineteenth century efforts to find scientific proof for life after death. Parapsychology includes the study of mind-to-mind communication (telepathy), the ability to perceive hidden objects and events (clairvoyance), and the ability to move objects by use of mental power alone (psychokinesis). Psychic studies were first organized in 1882 by the Society for Psychical Research in London, and an American society began three years later. First published in 1902, *Human Personality and its Survival of Bodily Death* by Frederic W. H. Myers has been called a classic in the field of psychical research. Myers gives evidence for survival of bodily death and communication with the "dead." From a vast number of case histories, he reported instances where sleeping people were seen somewhere else by other people, or their waking from dreams with previously unknown information. He cited occasions when the dead have been seen and described by people who had never seen them in life. He related cases of telepathic communication and "out-of-body" experiences. He concluded that there is something in the physical body that can leave it and this could be called the "soul" or "spirit."[224] Thomas Alva Edison, one of the greatest inventors in history, gave serious thought to creating a machine for communicating with the "dead."[225] Two different teams of researchers, one in the U.S. and the other in Germany, have both developed electronic devices that let them communicate with the dead. "This is undeniable proof that there is life after death," says Dr. Ernst Senkowski, professor of physics at the Technical College of Bingen, West Germany.[226]

In the CIA, the very word "parapsychology" is classified and any CIA report that mentions "psi," which refers to the whole range of phenomena, is automatically classified top secret or higher.[227] Many scientists believe that findings in parapsychology can be used to manipulate the minds of others.[228] In 1976, parapsychology research received direct support from CIA director George Bush.[229] Much of the current research on ESP involves out-of-body experiences, especially remote viewing—the ability to leave one's physical body and visit distant places.[230] Congressman Charles Rose of North Carolina, a member of the House Select Committee on Intelligence, has attended classified demonstrations of remote viewing arranged by the CIA. "I've seen some incredible examples of remote viewing so much so that we ought to pay close attention to developments in this field," says Congressman Rose.[231]

COMMENTARY: The essence of who and what we really are as spirit-soul is eternal and not subject to death but the physical body and material mind are. Bodily feelings and sensations disappear. The body decays and disintegrates. This dissolution is not really death, but the separation of an admixture of the soul (a unit of Consciousness) from matter (the body). One "dies" out of one realm and is born into another. One leaves the material world through "death" and is born into the realm of spirit. The basis and foundation of Reality is that All is Spirit and All is Consciousness. Consciousness is the substance of all things. The world and everything and everyone in it is an appearance in Consciousness. The term "Holy Spirit" means that Spirit is Holy because it is conscious and of the Supreme Consciousness and Spirit that is God. *"The last enemy that shall be destroyed is death."* (I Corinthians 15:26) The Truth is known and understood from within as an inner knowing and realization in Consciousness.

SECTION 18

Drugs

Drugs, including LSD and marijuana, have been tested alone and in combination with hypnosis on knowing and unknowing subjects by the CIA and other government intelligence agencies in order to find reliable ways to control the mind and human behavior.[232] Consciousness-altering drugs have been an important part of many religions for centuries.[233] In the Vedas, holy books written in India between 2000 and 1400 B.C., the god Siva is said to have brought marijuana from the Himalayas for man's benefit. A liquid preparation called "bhang" was described in the 10th century as the "food of the gods."[234] The peoples of Africa and the Indians of South America have used a variety of psychoactive drugs. The Incas of Peru chewed the leaves of the sacred coca plants.[235] The Indians of North America believed that the visions produced by the plant drugs were glimpses of a world on a different plane of reality, inhabited by spirits who provided useful information.[236] In every part of the world, almost all communities had their medicine men, witch doctors or shamans, selected primarily for their ability to communicate with the spirits. To visit the spirit world, the medicine man entered a state of trance, and this was frequently accomplished with the help of drugs. His function was to bring back useful information for his people.[237] Historical evidence links the use of certain plant drugs with the ability to practice divination. Travelers, missionaries and colonial administrators over the past century and a half have relayed in letters and memoirs countless stories of witch doctors accurately describing what was happening in distant places or correctly forecasting future events.[238] The plant drugs are capable of liberating psychic abilities in certain individuals, and it is for this reason they come under attack by Church and State.

COMMENTARY: The drug trade is controlled and operated by aristocratic families of the ruling class elite. The vast sums of money that are laundered by the banking establishment props up the corrupt financial system. In mid-2000, the Taliban began to eradicate opium production in Afghanistan. This decimated a huge cash flow. Afghanistan produced more than 70% of the world's heroin. War was the answer to restore and protect the profitable opium production. The trade in drugs, gold, silver and other precious metals, diamonds and other gems, oil and now information is the backbone of the merchant-finance-capitalist system. It's BIG business operating with the complicity of BIG government under the control of the ruling class elite. Government intelligence agencies were established primarily to protect the wealth and financial interests of these ruling class families and their heirs to perpetuate their control over the masses.

MIND CONTROL IS BEING USED ON AN UNSUSPECTING PUBLIC. MIND CONTROL IS BEING USED ON AN UNSUSPECTING PUBLIC.
MIND CONTROL IS BEING USED ON AN UNSUSPECTING PUBLIC. MIND CONTROL IS BEING USED ON AN UNSUSPECTING PUBLIC.
MIND CONTROL IS BEING USED ON AN UNSUSPECTING PUBLIC. MIND CONTROL IS BEING USED ON AN UNSUSPECTING PUBLIC.
MIND CONTROL IS BEING USED ON AN UNSUSPECTING PUBLIC. MIND CONTROL IS BEING USED ON AN UNSUSPECTING PUBLIC.
MIND CONTROL IS BEING USED ON AN UNSUSPECTING PUBLIC. MIND CONTROL IS BEING USED ON AN UNSUSPECTING PUBLIC.
MIND CONTROL IS BEING USED ON AN UNSUSPECTING PUBLIC. MIND CONTROL IS BEING USED ON AN UNSUSPECTING PUBLIC.
MIND CONTROL IS BEING USED ON AN UNSUSPECTING PUBLIC. MIND CONTROL IS BEING USED ON AN UNSUSPECTING PUBLIC.
MIND CONTROL IS BEING USED ON AN UNSUSPECTING PUBLIC. MIND CONTROL IS BEING USED ON AN UNSUSPECTING PUBLIC.
MIND CONTROL IS BEING USED ON AN UNSUSPECTING PUBLIC. MIND CONTROL IS BEING USED ON AN UNSUSPECTING PUBLIC.
MIND CONTROL IS BEING USED ON AN UNSUSPECTING PUBLIC. MIND CONTROL IS BEING USED ON AN UNSUSPECTING PUBLIC.
MIND CONTROL IS BEING USED ON AN UNSUSPECTING PUBLIC. MIND CONTROL IS BEING USED ON AN UNSUSPECTING PUBLIC.
MIND CONTROL IS BEING USED ON AN UNSUSPECTING PUBLIC. MIND CONTROL IS BEING USED ON AN UNSUSPECTING PUBLIC.
MIND CONTROL IS BEING USED ON AN UNSUSPECTING PUBLIC. MIND CONTROL IS BEING USED ON AN UNSUSPECTING PUBLIC.
MIND CONTROL IS BEING USED ON AN UNSUSPECTING PUBLIC. MIND CONTROL IS BEING USED ON AN UNSUSPECTING PUBLIC.
MIND CONTROL IS BEING USED ON AN UNSUSPECTING PUBLIC. MIND CONTROL IS BEING USED ON AN UNSUSPECTING PUBLIC.
MIND CONTROL IS BEING USED ON AN UNSUSPECTING PUBLIC. MIND CONTROL IS BEING USED ON AN UNSUSPECTING PUBLIC.
MIND CONTROL IS BEING USED ON AN UNSUSPECTING PUBLIC. MIND CONTROL IS BEING USED ON AN UNSUSPECTING PUBLIC.
MIND CONTROL IS BEING USED ON AN UNSUSPECTING PUBLIC. MIND CONTROL IS BEING USED ON AN UNSUSPECTING PUBLIC.
MIND CONTROL IS BEING USED ON AN UNSUSPECTING PUBLIC. MIND CONTROL IS BEING USED ON AN UNSUSPECTING PUBLIC.
MIND CONTROL IS BEING USED ON AN UNSUSPECTING PUBLIC. MIND CONTROL IS BEING USED ON AN UNSUSPECTING PUBLIC.

SECTION 19
The Secret of Marijuana

Throughout history, marijuana has been used to treat dozens of different diseases and conditions.[239] Chinese Emperor Shen Nung classified it in the *Herbal*, an equivalent of *the U.S. Pharmacopoeia* as an important medicine at about 2730 B.C. and taught his people how to grow it.[240] In the 15th century in India, it was believed to have numerous medical virtues. Documents from the 1500's show that English herbalists were using it as medicine, as were folk healers in Poland, Russia and Lithuania. During the 17th and 18th centuries, there were more references to it in medical texts. Between 1839 and 1900, there were more than one hundred published studies of marijuana as a medicine.[241] Potential medical uses include controlling nausea and vomiting caused by cancer chemotherapy, treatment of glaucoma by reducing excessive pressure within the eye, management of muscular spasms, control of epileptic seizures, treatment of asthma by increasing the diameter of the air passages of the lungs, relief of pain, treatment of migraine, treatment of anorexia nervosa by stimulating the appetite, anti-anxiety and sleep-inducing effects, treatment of depression, treatment of alcoholism and opiate dependence, reduction of high blood pressure.[242]

The American Medical Association has maintained a position on marijuana closely allied to that of the Federal Bureau of Narcotics. *The Journal of the American Medical Association* disregards as "unscientific" any study that does not demonstrate marijuana to be a "menace."[243] In their 1967 statement, the Committee on Alcoholism and Drug Dependence of the American Medical Association began with the assertion that "cannabis (marijuana) has no known use in medical practice in most countries of the world, including the United States."[244] In 1937, members of the Committee on Legislative Activities of the American Medical Association wrote in protesting the impending Marijuana Tax Act: "There is positively no evidence to indicate the abuse of cannabis as a medicinal agent or to show that its medicinal use is leading to the development of cannabis addiction."[245] In June 1980, the UNIMED Pharmaceutical Company applied to the Food and Drug Administration for approval to market THC, the active component of marijuana, under the trade name "Marinol."[246]

A major effect of the 1937 Marijuana Tax Act was to drive prices up for marijuana to make its cultivation and distribution profitable.[247] Where a plant drug can be exploited commercially, its use has been encouraged. The opium trade was encouraged by commercial interests in Western nations, particularly Great Britain. The League of Nations Opium Committee meeting in Geneva in 1925 was called "The Smugglers' Reunion."[248] Governments are the real drug pushers. Harassment and prosecution are reserved for those who enter the field without approval.[249] You will recall that secret knowledge is the basis of all power. Ruling elites arise and maintain their power through secret knowledge. Their power erodes as their secret knowledge is transformed into scientific knowledge and disappears when it becomes common knowledge.[250] You know that information can be controlled. You know that people can be led to believe something that is not true, especially when that information is presented by an accepted and respected authority. People keep secrets and lie when they are afraid and have something to hide. Marijuana holds a secret. Marijuana has a long history of ceremonial use in religion among the peoples of Africa, South America and India.[251] The Sufis, a mystical Islamic sect, continue to use marijuana in the traditional shamanist way to enter deeper levels of mind in order to gain access to useful information.[252] Marijuana serves as a guide to psychic areas of the mind which can then be re-entered without it.[253] This is the primary reason for the campaign against marijuana because the knowledge gained from its proper use challenges fundamental beliefs held by Western civilization and the power and authority of Church and State.

"Often beliefs that we hold are never called into question; when they are not, it is relatively easy for us to lose sight of why we hold them," says psychologist Elliot Aronson in *The Social Animal*.[254] Our beliefs are often based on something other than personal experience. Beliefs acquired during childhood indoctrination at home, school and church often masquerade as knowledge. Such indoctrination means that the individual takes on conclusions of others instead of arriving at his own. We tend to protect what we believe and unconsciously filter out information we don't want to receive. Most of us are programmed without being aware of it. A child learns that his needs will more likely be met if he conforms to what is expected of him. Society and its institutions teach and reward conformity and obedience to authority. What this does is discourage the individual from developing the capacity to think for himself and it also discourages any serious challenge to authority.[255]

COMMENTARY: In the 1933 novel *Lost Horizon*, author James Hinton writes that the 300 year old High Lama of Shangri-La, a lamasery high in the mountains of Tibet, follows a regimen of "drug taking and deep breathing exercises". It is the reason for the High Lama's longevity. *"His mind remained so extraordinarily clear that he even embarked upon a study of certain mystic practices that the Indians call yoga, and which are based upon various special methods of breathing."* The use of naturally occurring plant drugs as a Holy Sacrament to enter deeper levels of mind has a long history in the practice of religion all over the world. Artists often hide significant information in their work that would be too dangerous to disclose openly and attract the attention and wrath of the Church and State. The 1965 novel *Dune* by Frank Herbert, the 1984 movie adaptation directed by David Lynch and the 2000 TV mini-series is another example. The spice "Melange" expands Consciousness, prolongs life and is vital to space travel. The Spacing Guild and its Navigators, who the spice has mutated over time, use the spice which gives them the ability to "fold" space — travel to any part of the Universe without moving. The spice "Melange" is a metaphor for marijuana. Secret knowledge is one reason why its use comes under attack. Another reason is that its medicinal benefits are a threat to the profits of the pharmaceutical cartel. And a third reason is the massive unaccounted for amounts of cash generated for the banking establishment and the ruling class elite from its distribution and sale that makes continuing the charade profitable.

SECTION 20
The Origin of Man

When Charles Darwin's *Origin of Species* was published in 1859, there was considerable opposition to the whole idea of evolution because it challenged the Biblical story of Creation. The controversy continues to this day. Evolution and Darwinism, however, do not mean the same thing even though they are often misunderstood as being the same. Evolution is a process of change. Evolution of life over a very long period of time is a fact based on evidence from geology, paleontology, molecular biology and other scientific disciplines. Darwinism, on the other hand, is a theory that tries to explain evolution, and despite many efforts, it has not been proved. Darwin believed that new species evolved out of existing ones, that fish evolved into amphibians, amphibians into reptiles, reptiles into birds, and ultimately man evolved from an ape-like ancestor as the result of gradually accumulated improvements. But fossils showing key transitions from one life form to another have never been found. The fossil record often reveals a pattern of evolutionary leaps rather than the gradual changes Darwin foresaw.[256]

The appearance of modern man on this planet was sudden.[257] Darwin and the evolutionists found no Missing Link between man and the ape because man is not the evolutionary culmination of the primates.[258] The origin of Man described in Genesis is an allegorical explanation of what happened. Allegory is a way to describe something that is profound in terms of something simple. It is a symbolic representation of fact; it is not the fact itself. A literal interpretation of the allegory makes the allegory more important than what it was meant to represent.[259] Fundamentalists make this error. Both the Bible and evolutionists are incomplete in their explanation of Man's origin.

The name "Adam" is derived from the Babylonian-Sumerian name for "human species". "Adam" meant man as a race. The nakedness of Adam was their lacking physical bodies. Man arrived on this planet in spirit form in a series of migrations. As a result, some are older in experience than others. Man came here to learn about creation and the responsibilities that go with the ability to create by the power of thought. God creates by thought and so does Man. Man was to experience a finite world and know physical limitations in order to appreciate the lack of limitations and the responsibilities it carries. Man observed the developing life forms evolving on the planet. Fascinated and preoccupied with sex, a group created physical bodies by the power of thought or by invading the bodies of animals, cohabited with animals and taught those practices to others. The crossing of Man's spirit with animals produced a race of hybrids. Animals and men became interchangeable. There were divine animals and beastly divinities. The Sphinx with a lion's body and human head is symbolic of this sequence in Man's history. The 18th Chapter of Leviticus, verses 22-30 refers to this period of sodomy when Man cohabited with animals. The Fall of Man was Man's descent into flesh and the spiritual degeneration that resulted. It became necessary to cleanse the Earth as told in the allegory of Noah and the Flood. Life forms existing in purity were preserved. Monstrosities and abominations were destroyed. Those who perished physically were not dead spiritually. They were simply minus the physical body they had been inhabiting. However, their consciousness had been contaminated, making a Plan of Redemption necessary to separate Man and beast and return both to their original status. One lifetime would not be enough to straighten out what had happened. Many lifetimes would be necessary to eradicate the beastly traits in Man. By overcoming the weaknesses and desires of the flesh, Man cleanses himself of that which defiled him and thus works his way back to his original consciousness and the return home to the spiritual world.[260]

"Why think ye that flesh developed a mechanism of reasoning brain if not for high employment? If ye were rewarded in this single earthly life according to your just deserts, verily would flesh defeat its mortal purpose. I adjure you to remember that ye do sow what ye wouldst reap, ye do reap what ye have sown, not alone in one life but in countless other lives whose formings are but memories. Lives without number have ye led; Spirit goeth into flesh and Spirit cometh out. Harken and I teach you as I spake unto the prophets: observe and be wise, for it behooveth you to know that others have trod the Path before you and would call to you now from the heights of their attainings. Man cometh and goeth in his flesh that he may learn lessons, verily of his flesh, verily of his Spirit. Did I not say unto men: Elias hath come already, and they understood me not, though I spake of John the Baptist? How spake I then of John the Baptist as Elias come again, if Spirit goeth not into flesh times and again, and cometh out times, and times and one more? Of this did I minister; of such did I instruct; But the spirits of men were perverse in that generation even as of yours; they did say, He speaketh to us of madness. Behold, I spake no madness: I spake in the truth, but they feared the truth even as they did fear me who brought it to them, in that I brought it. Arise and be wise: put off the ragged garment of ignorance; know the secret of life's mystery." This is a condensed version of information contained in chapter 6 of *The Golden Scripts* published by Fellowship Press, Inc. of Noblesville, Indiana as recorded by William Dudley Pelley in the 1930s. Pelley investigated the principles of survival of the human spirit and cultivated his own psychic abilities. The body of work that came to be *The Golden Scripts* and the Soulcraft Teaching was dictated to him.

"Know ye, beloved, that in the beginning man had no image by physical body. Intellect was. Men were created Spirit by Spirit. Know ye that intellect sought flesh for a purpose. Spirit as spirit hath no identity; only after long experience on planes of matter doth spirit feel its essence. Thus cometh identity: through trial and through error, through life as mortal being. Man was divine from the beginning, a thought-force of the Father, knowing good and evil, creating no material thing without a loving purpose. I tell you, man was to rule as god over systems of planets one day to be within his control. Yet did man embrace his opportunity to make himself god of earth-creation without gaining to experience; thus did he fill the earth with his thought-forms. What think ye is the meaning of the Fable of Sodom? Having monsters by his making, he did have of them whoredoms; he did bring upon his species an appalling catastrophe. Thus correcteth he a wrong through his fleshly visitations, that by overcoming the weaknesses and desires of his flesh, he cleanseth himself of that which defiled him. Thus hath he known earth-life, aeon unto aeon, form unto form, body unto body."[261]

Man is a blend of indigenous primates and the spiritual beings who arrived on this planet and adopted the primate physical body. They cohabited with the indigenous primates and their offspring was the first man. The inheritance of animal traits still lingers in man, making so many spiritual beings beastly in their temperaments and behaviors. Only through much instruction and experience in all stations of human life could man earn back realization of his original spiritual consciousness. Inherent in man is much of his lost heritage, but he has been forbidden by Thought Forces superior to him to use it until he has reached that time when he is so spiritually balanced and developed that he can never again employ his knowledge malevolently or selfishly. That time is close at hand.[262] Ancient mystery religions taught that man had the power to tap the natural forces from higher spheres. This is The Force in *Star Wars*. A 1972 Defense Intelligence Agency study, originally classified top secret but released in 1978, concludes that "the powers of the subconscious mind are vastly superior to those of the conscious."[263] Think of your subconscious mind as your link with The Force. Now imagine your conscious mind directing the power of the Force. "The unleashing of this force within you is a mighty torrent; it is a molecular energy of a speed and variation encompassed by no human brain in concept; it is Force Triumphant, striking him dead who hath not the power to use it aright."[264]

COMMENTARY: The "Book of Enoch" tells the story of the fallen angels and the origin of demons. Two hundred "Watchers," as they were called, fell into matter, attracted by the desire for sensual enjoyment. Their offspring were a hybrid mixture of an Earthly species with a celestial one. The giants that resulted, what the Bible calls the "Nefilim," had voracious appetites and cravings. When no longer in a physical body, their materially contaminated consciousness was demonic. They became the evil spirits who corrupt and oppress mankind. Once part of the Bible, the "Book of Enoch," fell into disfavor with powerful theologians and was omitted because of its descriptions of the nature and deeds of the fallen angels. It was once considered part of the apocryphal writings by the early church fathers. The word "apocryphal" is derived from the Greek and means "secret" or "hidden". It was considered too secret to be made available to the general population. Remember that secret knowledge is the basis of all power. Our judgment is only as good as the quality and accuracy of our information, and information can be controlled.

According to Sumerian history, the Anunnaki descended from the sky in winged vehicles, created Man by modifying a pre-existing primate species and established civilization. Sumerian accounts say that originally Man was not as modern man, but a human hybrid, modified in a series of genetic enhancements, the result of which was modern man. Ancient societies reported contact with extraterrestrial and higher dimensional beings along with descriptions of their aerial vehicles that parallel modern descriptions of UFOs. The scriptures of India speak of 400,000 different varieties of human life on various planets, varying widely in physical form and mental power. Many different humanoid races are said to live in parallel worlds and higher dimensions within the Earth, on its surface and in the atmosphere surrounding it. There are races that are ego-centered and not dedicated to the service of God who tend to be materialistic, attracted to the development of technology and the exploitation of mental powers for selfish ends. Demons incarnate on Earth in the attempt to take over and rule the planet. Their counterparts, the angels and demigods, incarnate to assist the Plan for Man's Redemption, to show Man the way home to the spiritual world.

In the legends of people around the world, there are accounts of non-human races, some divine and some demonic. Sumerian records show that celestial beings the Sumerians called "gods" came from the sky and ruled as Earth's first kings. These beings mated with humans and employed genetic engineering to create primitive workers they could use as slaves in exploiting the resources of the planet. The first human kings were the offspring of these "gods" who mated with Earth women, forming an aristocracy as an intermediary between the gods and Man. Some ancient gods were depicted as "blue-skinned" or "blue-blooded," giving rise to the concept of "royal-blood" and the breeding practices of the aristocracy in forming political alliances.

References to "serpent-gods" and "flying dragons" are found in the mythology of many cultures around the world. A non-human race, the Nagas, described as having a serpent form is mentioned in the scriptures of India. In talking about the oral history of his people, Zulu shaman Credo Mutwa says that man was created by a reptilian species that came from the sky. In Chinese mythology, the celestial dragon was said to be the father of the first dynasty of divine emperors. In the Garden of Eden, the serpent stood upright on two legs and could speak. According to the Bible, the serpent was "the shrewdest of the creatures made by God," implying a developed intellect and will beyond a mere animal form. The ancients believed that these "gods" who evolved differently elsewhere, were reptilian creatures who arrived to establish a colony on Earth. The Jewish Encyclopedia says that the "coats of skin" that clothed Adam and Eve were made from the skin of the serpent.

As the story goes, a human-reptilian hybrid formed the priesthood, serving as intermediary between Man and the serpent-gods. Only the priesthood could approach the "gods". The "badge of the priesthood" was a patch of scaly skin often on the chest. This sign of "divinity" is also mentioned in the scriptures of India as a "coat of armor, like a divine being". In the case of a demonic serpent species, the identification of a negative entity would be reflected in what was expected of the worshipers. In addition to the command to kill, enslave and destroy, there were both animal and human sacrifice in the Old Testament. *"Sanctify unto me all the first-born, whatsoever openeth the womb among the children of Israel, both of man and of beast is mine."* (Exodus 13:2) Human beings and animals were sacrificed for the blood-lust of these creatures whose history is intertwined with that of mankind. This is the source for the man-eating dragons that are prevalent in so many cultures. This is also the source of stories about the blood-letting associated with devil worship and Satanism. On the other hand, a divine reptilian species was credited with establishing civilization and bringing many benefits. Quetzacoatl brought civilization to Mexico; his opposite, Tezcatlipoca brought discord, destruction and human sacrifice. One species of "serpent-god" represented divine attributes and help for Man's spiritual growth and expansion of consciousness, while the other species represented demonic attributes and opposition to Man's rising to the platform of God Consciousness.

MIND CONTROL IS BEING USED ON AN UNSUSPECTING PUBLIC. MIND CONTROL IS BEING USED ON AN UNSUSPECTING PUBLIC.
MIND CONTROL IS BEING USED ON AN UNSUSPECTING PUBLIC. MIND CONTROL IS BEING USED ON AN UNSUSPECTING PUBLIC.
MIND CONTROL IS BEING USED ON AN UNSUSPECTING PUBLIC. MIND CONTROL IS BEING USED ON AN UNSUSPECTING PUBLIC.
MIND CONTROL IS BEING USED ON AN UNSUSPECTING PUBLIC. MIND CONTROL IS BEING USED ON AN UNSUSPECTING PUBLIC.
MIND CONTROL IS BEING USED ON AN UNSUSPECTING PUBLIC. MIND CONTROL IS BEING USED ON AN UNSUSPECTING PUBLIC.
MIND CONTROL IS BEING USED ON AN UNS

SECTION 21

The Powers of
the Subconscious Mind

BEING USED ON AN UNSUSPECTING PUBLIC.
BEING USED ON AN UNSUSPECTING PUBLIC.
BEING USED ON AN UNSUSPECTING PUBLIC.
USED ON AN UNSUSPECTING PUBLIC.
USED ON AN UNSUSPECTING PUBLIC.
USED ON AN UNSUSPECTING PUBLIC.
USED ON AN UNSUSPECTING PUBLIC.
USPECTING PUBLIC.
USPECTING PUBLIC.
USPECTING PUBLIC.
MIND CONTROL IS BEING USED ON AN UNSUSPECTING PUBLIC. MIND CONTROL IS BEING USED ON AN UNSUSPECTING PUBLIC.
MIND CONTROL IS BEING USED ON AN UNSUSPECTING PUBLIC. MIND CONTROL IS BEING USED ON AN UNSUSPECTING PUBLIC.
MIND CONTROL IS BEING USED ON AN UNSUSPECTING PUBLIC. MIND CONTROL IS BEING USED ON AN UNSUSPECTING PUBLIC.

The great secret possessed by the great men of all ages has been their ability to release the powers of their subconscious mind.[265] Your subconscious mind accepts as true whatever your conscious mind believes to be true. What the conscious mind believes, the subconscious acts on. It works like programming a computer. You feed information into a computer, and the computer acts on it. However, if the information you feed into the computer is wrong, it still acts on it! If you give yourself incorrect information or if others give you incorrect information, the memory banks of your subconscious mind do not correct the error but act on it! The conscious mind cannot be controlled by the suggestions of someone else when those suggestions are contrary to what you know from your own experience. But the subconscious mind is amenable to control by suggestion, by you and others. The subconscious mind can be manipulated without conscious awareness as evidenced by the phenomenon of subliminal perception. The most effective way to protect yourself from subconscious manipulation is to be aware of how it works. The techniques used to enslave the mind are the same used to free it. This amounts to re-programming the subconscious mind to break past conditioning and restore itself to its healthy functioning. To do this requires an understanding of the interaction between the conscious mind and the subconscious.

Meditation is a method of clearing the mind as preparation for a mental discipline of a much higher order. The principles behind meditation are the same as those for mental programming: distraction and repetition. Distraction focuses the attention of the conscious mind on one or more of the five senses in order to stop all thoughts and mental activity. The subconscious mind is thus susceptible to suggestion and programming. Repetition of a mantra, a word or several words, or focusing your attention on something visual, real or imaginary, is the program. The tools of the conscious mind are words (spoken, written and thought) and pictures and sounds. The conscious mind discriminates, evaluates, accepts or rejects. The subconscious responds to the suggestions your conscious mind gives to it.[266] The power of suggestion is the power of belief. It is an act of faith. Jesus said: "According to your faith be it unto you" (Matthew 9:29). This is the foundation of all mental programming. "Whatsoever ye shall ask in prayer, believing, ye shall receive."[267]

Think back to the times when you have been upset and without thinking you automatically began to breathe in deeply and rapidly to calm down and get yourself back together. Now breathe in slowly and deeply and exhale in the same fashion, slowly and deeply. You are feeling more relaxed. Pantanjali, an Indian sage who codified the practice of yoga in the second century A.D., wrote that control of thoughts and emotions is linked to breath control. Modern scientists are proving what ancient philosophers often believed to be true: that breathing affects our mental, emotional, and physical well-being. Dr. Rudolph Ballentine of the Himalayan Institute, a yogic research center in Pennsylvania, says that "breathing is directly related in a very strategic way to the functioning of the internal organs, the emotions and the mind." Changing the way you breathe can change the way your brain works, giving you conscious control over your blood pressure, metabolism, emotions, brain waves and mind.[268]

Now go back to early childhood experience and see yourself as a tiny tot long before school age, even before you could speak, untouched and unspoiled by the adult world. Imagine yourself as a tiny tot romping around in the nature of the life of the outdoors, frolicking through the tall grass. As you enjoy the warmth of the sunlight pour down on your face, across your forehead, your cheeks, and your eyelids, drinking in this warmth as it penetrates your body with a beautiful, peaceful, comfortable, warm feeling within. Now breathe in slowly and deeply and exhale in the same fashion, slowly and deeply. As you gradually become aware of your healthy, rhythmic breathing pattern, as you breathe in slowly and deeply in the healthiest possible fashion, you slow

down your body functions and your mind because you're always in command, you're always in control over the healthy faculties of mind to maintain perfect health of mind and body. Thus you have choice and because you have choice, your intuitive level of your subconscious mind will only accept that which it finds perfectly comfortable and acceptable for perfect health of mind and body. Thus you will not allow any one thing or any one person or any one environment or part thereof to interfere with your choice and your desire for perfect health of mind and body. Thus you maintain complete communication between your conscious and subconscious mind to fulfill this health program and all these positive health goals that you are setting for yourself from this time forth.

COMMENTARY: The last paragraph above is from the audio "Personal Comfort Training" developed by Samuel J. Jacobson, a hypnotist, researcher and consultant to the medical profession for more than 20 years. The audio was developed over a period of 11 years for use in private practice for patients referred by physicians in cases of chronic pain, neurological disorders, emotional problems and respiratory ailments. This unique audio helps the listener identify deeper, more relaxed levels of mind in order to enter them at will and function in them for extended periods of time. It is a health program that speaks directly to the subconscious. Repeated daily listening will in time help break negative programming and conditioning. For more information about this audio, visit the website: www.personalcomforttraining.com

The subconscious mind is the storehouse of all memories, emotions, habits and conditioned behavior. It also has control over all the functions, conditions and sensations of the body. It is a mighty force that brings good or bad depending on how it is used. Therefore, it is important to understand how to use it intelligently and consciously. The subconscious operates by suggestion, given to you or by you. Once given a suggestion, it will seek to bring about conditions and circumstances that will make the suggestion a reality. The subconscious is like a garden that creates reality from the seed of thought. It acts on the most predominant thought behind which there is the most belief. Repeating the thought and energizing it with faith and conviction is like watering the garden. Visualize the ideal condition desired in every detail and hold firmly the mental picture with faith in the inevitability of the desired result. This creates a blueprint or matrix for the subconscious to follow and propels it into action. Thought plus faith and conviction lead to manifestation. Doubt, fear and worry delay it. Whatever the mind dwells upon manifests according to the repetition and intensity of feeling behind the thought projected. Habitual thoughts and emotions that are negative limit our capabilities and bring us what we don't want. Dissolve the negative by implanting a positive program to override the negative. An attitude of joy, gratitude and expectation hasten the manifestation of what you desire. Thinking the right thoughts is the basis of all accomplishment. Fear is the negative use of faith. Fear prompts the subconscious to manifest what is feared. Refuse to accept any negative circumstance as final. Faith is the way to overcome negative thoughts and emotions. *"All things are possible to him who believeth."* (Mark 9:23) All things begin with faith, allowing one to rise above every adverse condition and circumstance. There is nothing that a strong faith and noble purpose cannot accomplish. *"According to your faith, be it unto you."* (Matthew 9:29)

The conscious mind deals with the five senses and the external world. It analyzes, records and files pleasure-pain sensations and their cause in the attempt to avoid pain and maximize pleasure. What is too painful or traumatic for the conscious mind gets buried in the subconscious as a complex, a phobia, an obsession, a conditioned response sustained and energized by negative thinking and emotions. Break the habit of negative thinking and emotions by gradually building a new conditioned response. Fighting a bad habit intensifies it. The only way to overcome it is by replacing it with its opposite. Abandon each negative thought and emotion as it arises. Keep digging up the weeds in the garden of your subconscious and you will find fewer and fewer until they are all gone. We live in an ocean of consciousness, invisible and formless yet pliable, that manifests what we think and say into it.

Meditation is the means to purifying one's consciousness and experiencing conscious Awareness of God. The mind is restless and difficult to control. Thoughts come and go in an endless stream. The mind pulls our attention down into it and we get lost in our thinking. We are controlled by our thinking and not by our Awareness. We think with our emotions and get lost in them. Meditation is the way to stabilize the mind and stop it from wandering. Still the mind and separate from it so that you can observe your Awareness as separate from your thoughts. You are not your thoughts. You are the observer of your thoughts and the Awareness behind them. It will help to practice looking at the world as if you were someone else, a third party observing your thoughts, feelings and actions objectively. Transform your mind into an awareness beyond the limitations of a conditioned ego that lives in the imagination. Habits of thinking, feeling and perception dictate how we respond to the outside world and everyday situations. These habits are programmed behavior – the results of repetition. A single thought, feeling or action makes an impression upon the mind; repeated often enough, that impression establishes a conditioned response. Meditation is the means by which conditioned responses are dissolved.

There is a significant difference between the meditative state of mind and the hypnotic state of mind. The hypnotic state of mind is a trance state where the mind is blank and there is no conscious mental activity. It is a twilight state, just like that state of mind when we are drifting off to sleep at night or just awakening in the morning. It is in this state of mind where one is the most susceptible to the influence of suggestion and more receptive to mental programming than at any other time. The attention of the conscious mind is focused on one or more of the five senses in order to induce a state of single-pointed attention and heightened suggestibility. The meditative state of mind, on the other hand, although also a trance state induced by single-pointed attention, is a heightened state of awareness and differs significantly in this respect: in meditation, one is in full, total and complete conscious awareness, whereas in hypnosis, one is unconscious even while awake. Meditation leads one out of the trance of hypnosis, leading to the transformation of Consciousness. *"And be not conformed to this world: but be ye transformed by the renewing of your mind, that ye may prove what is that good, and acceptable, and perfect, will of God."* (Romans 12:2)

MIND CONTROL IS BEING USED ON AN UNSUSPECTING PUBLIC. MIND CONTROL IS BEING USED ON AN UNSUSPECTING PUBLIC.
MIND CONTROL IS BEING USED ON AN UNSUSPECTING PUBLIC. MIND CONTROL IS BEING USED ON AN UNSUSPECTING PUBLIC.
MIND CONTROL IS BEING USED ON AN UNSUSPECTING PUBLIC. MIND CONTROL IS BEING USED ON AN UNSUSPECTING PUBLIC.
MIND CONTROL IS BEING USED ON AN UNSUSPECTING PUBLIC. MIND CONTROL IS BEING USED ON AN UNSUSPECTING PUBLIC.
MIND CONTROL IS BEING USED ON AN UNSUSPECTING PUBLIC. MIND CONTROL IS BEING USED ON AN UNSUSPECTING PUBLIC.
MIND CONTROL IS BEING USED ON AN UN

SECTION 22
Kali Yuga

BEING USED ON AN UNSUSPECTING PUBLIC.
BEING USED ON AN UNSUSPECTING PUBLIC.
BEING USED ON AN UNSUSPECTING PUBLIC.
IS BEING USED ON AN UNSUSPECTING PUBLIC.
IS BEING USED ON AN UNSUSPECTING PUBLIC.
IS BEING USED ON AN UNSUSPECTING PUBLIC.
IS BEING USED ON AN UNSUSPECTING PUBLIC.
IS BEING USED ON AN UNSUSPECTING PUBLIC.
MIND CONTROL IS BEING USED ON AN UNSUSPECTING PUBLIC. MIND CONTROL IS BEING USED ON AN UNSUSPECTING PUBLIC.
MIND CONTROL IS BEING USED ON AN UNSUSPECTING PUBLIC. MIND CONTROL IS BEING USED ON AN UNSUSPECTING PUBLIC.
MIND CONTROL IS BEING USED ON AN UNSUSPECTING PUBLIC. MIND CONTROL IS BEING USED ON AN UNSUSPECTING PUBLIC.
MIND CONTROL IS BEING USED ON AN UNSUSPECTING PUBLIC. MIND CONTROL IS BEING USED ON AN UNSUSPECTING PUBLIC.
MIND CONTROL IS BEING USED ON AN UNSUSPECTING PUBLIC. MIND CONTROL IS BEING USED ON AN UNSUSPECTING PUBLIC.

In the book *1984*, George Orwell warns that people are in danger of losing their freedom of mind without being aware of it while it is happening because of psychological engineering. 1984 is here! "These are the times that try men's souls. The summer soldier and the sunshine patriot will, in this crisis, shrink from the service of his country; but he that stands it now, deserves the love and thanks of man and woman. Tyranny, like hell, is not easily conquered; yet we have this consolation with us; that the harder the conflict, the more glorious the triumph. What we obtain too cheap, we esteem too lightly; 'tis dearness only that gives everything its value. Heaven knows how to put a proper price upon its goods; and it would be strange indeed, if so celestial an article as 'Freedom' should not be highly rated."[269] Your rebellious brother who sought to make the earth-creation his, continues to pursue that aim. Using the instruments of government, rule through money, art, education, organized religion, science and technology, he seeks to enslave his brother by shackling his mind, thereby attempting to subvert his brother's birthright of knowledge. To the Hindu and Buddhist we approach the end of a cycle, the Kali Yuga or Black Age, a time of turmoil, upheaval and destruction. Sacred in ancient Egypt, the phoenix, a legendary bird, rose anew from its own ashes after being consumed by fire. It is a symbol of immortality, resurrection and regeneration.

"Life hath decreed man to walk in darkness for a period of his days that he might attain unto godhood through endurance. Man hath come to a crossroads in his sojourn on this planet; he hath come up from beast to see majesties eternal; he attaineth unto his heritage. Now I tell you he approacheth a crisis. That crisis is of me. I have said that I am come unto men to show them the way to make a great peace; lo, they do not wish peace; their skill of manufacture would vent itself in war. Man hath found himself the tool of caprice in matters having material ends. These things shall be changed. I say unto man: Beware, thou are not the creature of caprice that is in thee. Behold thou art heavenly, destined for eternity. Man hath arrived at the ending of a cycle: he cometh to accounting: I speak unto him saying: Lest thou destroy thyself, I prohibit abomination of art and of science; I prohibit thee from taking forces that are beyond thine understanding and making them instruments for the destruction of thy species. I give unto you benefits and ye use them not wisely; lo, I withdraw them unless ye are circumspect. Improve thine own spirit lest benefits allotted thee be wrested from thy hand. Man hath made himself lord over matter and shaped it to his ends; lo, he hath not made himself god of his own spirit. I come unto him to tell him that unless he seeth the Light and useth it, he is beastly again, and goeth down and not up. The world is at a crossroads. Blunder ye no longer! give up thy caprices! give up thy intent ever to defraud thy fellows by making your havocs among them for gain. Live peaceably, I tell you: come into the heritage of thine inventions for the good of thy race and not for its injury; follow not thine own conceits but raise up a standard unto Him who is Lord. The Father hath desired that man should learn lessons. He hath given man his increase, now he saith unto man: Prove by your behavior that ye have come to the anointment, rise up and be cleanly that ye merit the treasure. The Father hath said that verily an increase cometh unto man, but only that he merit it."[270]

COMMENTARY: In the Hindu cosmology, the term "Yuga" designates one of a four-age cycle of creation and destruction of the universe like the changing of seasons in which the Earth and the consciousness of mankind goes through gradual changes. From the Golden Age called "Satya Yuga" to the Dark Age of "Kali Yuga" there is a decline in religion, wisdom, knowledge, physical strength, stature and life span.

According to the Vedic scriptures of ancient India, the Kali Yuga, the age we live in, is a Dark Age where Man is mired in Materialism. In this consciousness people seek happiness in objects: people, places and things. However, the sages and scriptures of the world's religions say that true happiness can be found only within and not in the outer world. Once found within, it is then manifested in the outer world. A world in crisis, confusion, fear, anger, resentment, envy, hatred, cruelty, greed and general unhappiness is the outer or manifested expression in the physical, material world of inner, invisible causes in the collective consciousness of mankind under the influence of unseen forces. All is Consciousness. If you wish to change the outer expression of consciousness all that is necessary is to change the inner, invisible cause consciously by making an adjustment in Consciousness. "As within, so without" is a principle and law governing creation and the manifestation of form, environment, circumstances and events.

Though the Kali Yuga is a time of quarrel, confusion and chaos, it is also an opportunity for the transformation and upliftment of mankind. According to the Vedic scriptures of ancient India, there is a Golden Age period during Kali Yuga that promotes the awakening of spiritual consciousness in mankind. Those who disengage themselves from material consciousness rise above the influence of the material dimension.

MIND CONTROL IS BEING USED ON AN UNSUSPECTING PUBLIC. MIND CONTROL IS BEING USED ON AN UNSUSPECTING PUBLIC.
MIND CONTROL IS BEING USED ON AN UNSUSPECTING PUBLIC. MIND CONTROL IS BEING USED ON AN UNSUSPECTING PUBLIC.
MIND CONTROL IS BEING USED ON AN UNSUSPECTING PUBLIC. MIND CONTROL IS BEING USED ON AN UNSUSPECTING PUBLIC.
MIND CONTROL IS BEING USED ON AN UNSUSPECTING PUBLIC. MIND CONTROL IS BEING USED ON AN UNSUSPECTING PUBLIC.
MIND CONTROL IS BEING USED ON AN UNSUSPECTING PUBLIC. MIND CONTROL IS BEING USED ON AN UNSUSPECTING PUBLIC.
MIND CONTROL IS BEING USED ON AN UNS   ING USED ON AN UNSUSPECTING PUBLIC.
MIND CONTROL IS BEING USED ON AN UNS   ING USED ON AN UNSUSPECTING PUBLIC.
MIND CONTROL IS BEING USED ON AN UNS   ING USED ON AN UNSUSPECTING PUBLIC.
MIND CONTROL IS BEING USED ON AN UNS   ING USED ON AN UNSUSPECTING PUBLIC.
MIND CONTROL IS BEING USED ON AN UN   ING USED ON AN UNSUSPECTING PUBLIC.
MIND CONTROL IS BEING USED ON AN   ING USED ON AN UNSUSPECTING PUBLIC.
MIND CONTROL IS BEING USED ON AN   ING USED ON AN UNSUSPECTING PUBLIC.
MIND CONTROL IS BEING USED ON AN UNS   ING USED ON AN UNSUSPECTING PUBLIC.
MIND CONTROL IS BEING USED ON AN UNSUSPECTING PUBLIC. MIND CONTROL IS BEING USED ON AN UNSUSPECTING PUBLIC.
MIND CONTROL IS BEING USED ON AN UNSUSPECTING PUBLIC. MIND CONTROL IS BEING USED ON AN UNSUSPECTING PUBLIC.
MIND CONTROL IS BEING USED ON AN UNSUSPECTING PUBLIC. MIND CONTROL IS BEING USED ON AN UNSUSPECTING PUBLIC.
MIND CONTROL IS BEING USED ON AN UNSUSPECTING PUBLIC. MIND CONTROL IS BEING USED ON AN UNSUSPECTING PUBLIC.
MIND CONTROL IS BEING USED ON AN UNSUSPECTING PUBLIC. MIND CONTROL IS BEING USED ON AN UNSUSPECTING PUBLIC.
MIND CONTROL IS BEING USED ON AN UNSUSPECTING PUBLIC. MIND CONTROL IS BEING USED ON AN UNSUSPECTING PUBLIC.

Section 23
Conclusion

The missing dimension in world politics is the spiritual dimension. The problems of life cannot be solved by material means. Spiritual consciousness is the only solution to the problems and suffering of material existence. The majority of the population does not know who and what they really are. Because of this lack of knowledge, they are vulnerable to all manner of deception and manipulation. Most people misidentify themselves as the physical body, the mind and ego-personality. You have a body, but you are not the body. You have a mind, but you are not the mind. You have an ego-personality, but that is not who and what you really are. You are spirit-soul, an individual unit of consciousness – of God's Consciousness. Consciousness contaminated by matter misidentifies the temporary physical body, the mind and ego-personality as one's identity and thus becomes further entangled in material activities. Modern civilization is misdirected towards sense pleasure, the gratification of the bodily senses and the acquisition of wealth, power and prestige, the basis of material consciousness and a barrier to spiritual realization. Human life is meant for understanding spiritual values. Real knowledge is knowing yourself, who and what you are, who and what God is and our relationship to one another and to God. It is not possible to become peaceful and happy in the attempt to gratify the temporary material senses of the physical body and to seek personal ego-gratification. Spiritual life begins when you understand that you are not the body, not the mind, not the ego-personality, but spirit-soul and act on the basis of that knowledge and understanding.

The purpose of life is to become conscious of God and to live totally in that consciousness. The purpose of religion is to show the way to do that. However, there is a concerted effort to prevent the population from realizing

86

God Consciousness by various distractions and counterfeit knowledge. Our judgement is only as good as the quality and accuracy of our information and information can be controlled. There are those in high places who do not want to enlighten the population, but to enslave it. *"For we wrestle not against flesh and blood, but against principalities, against powers, against the rulers of the darkness of this world, against spiritual wickedness in high places."* (Ephesians 6:12)   Secret knowledge is the means by which mankind is subjected to tyranny and oppression. It is also the doorway to Liberation, Salvation, Enlightenment and the end of suffering.

The purpose of government is inexorably tied to the purpose of life. The sum of good government is knowledge of the purpose of life and the administration of society towards the fulfillment of that goal. If the men and women in leadership positions in the United States and elsewhere in the world do not know the objective of life, then they are not capable of administering a peaceful society. If, however, they do know and they do nothing to solve society's problems and do not seek to administer society for the highest good of all people equally, then what we see happening in the United States and throughout the world is the deliberate attempt to undermine the primary objective of life: the spiritual emancipation of mankind from the limitations and bondage of material consciousness.

It is necessary to purify one's consciousness to enter the spiritual kingdom of God and return home to the spiritual world. The highest goal of all religion is pure, devotional service and absolute unconditional surrender unto the Supreme Lord. *"And thou shalt love the Lord thy God with all thy heart, and with all thy soul, and with all thy mind, and with all thy strength: this is the first commandment. And the second is like, namely this, Thou shalt love thy neighbour as thyself. There is none other commandment greater than these."* (Mark 12:30-31)   God is Infinite Consciousness whereas the living entity is atomic in nature, a unit of God's Consciousness. Individual souls are tiny fragments of the Supreme Soul like the sparks of a fire. The living entity is simultaneously one with and different from God. The living entity is in one body; God is in all bodies. Therefore, to make distinctions between one living being and another on the basis of the material body is to see with material vision for the quality of the soul is the same in all bodies. God has expanded Himself as living beings to accept loving service from them. We are all members of the same family and meant to serve God with love and devotion in spiritual equality. This is true

87

oneness and unity in diversity. To see the same soul in all living beings is to see with the eyes of God.

The only difference of substance between one living being and another is the development of consciousness. Different varieties of life are evidence of different varieties of consciousness, the outer form being a vehicle for consciousness to grow and expand through experience in different forms. There is a wide variety of spirit life in different stages of growth and expansion of consciousness with the purpose of developing the individual unit of consciousness to complete realization of itself and its Source, culminating in the human stage of consciousness where realization of unity with the Universal Spirit of God and God Consciousness become possible.

"He that findeth his life shall lose it." (Matthew 10:39) The "me" you call yourself is totally conditioned by habit. The part of you that you call "I" and "Me" (your ego-personality) is programmed by society, its institutions and by your own thoughts, words and deeds. The "real" you, however, is hidden behind your conditioning. Everyone refers to himself and herself as "I" and "Me". You are a particular "I" and "Me" at a particular moment. With the next thought, the next emotion and the next moment, you are a different "I" and "Me". A multiplicity of "I's" and "Me's" make up the false ego. But the real you is changeless and eternal. It is your Awareness when the mind is silent and still. It is the "I AM," above, beyond, prior to and distinct from the mind, body and false ego. The "I AM" is the Christ of God in Man, the Divine center of Man's Consciousness, Pure Awareness, Pure Being, Pure Spirit. This is Man's original, Pure Consciousness. Its realization is the return to Innocence. It is how a child sees – without thinking, without judging, with "choiceless awareness," with "no mind." *"Whosoever shall not receive the kingdom of God as a little child, he shall not enter therein."* (Mark 10:15)

Self-Realization and not sense gratification is the purpose of life. Misidentifying one's self as the physical body, attachment to the physical body and the desire to gratify the bodily senses is the root cause of all suffering. Therefore, to end all suffering, transform material desires into spiritual desires and free the soul from the demands of the material senses centered in the mind. Those who learn self-control through self-discipline can end the suffering of material existence. Unless one learns to control the mind and senses, one cannot make any spiritual advancement. Modern culture and its preoccupation with sex encourages a bodily conception of life and greater entanglement in material consciousness so that the path to the spiritual world is blocked.

The mind absorbed in making plans for sense gratification is the cause of material bondage. Changes of mood, happiness and distress exist only in the mind. They are reflexes of the lower self, a programmed, conditioned response. The senses pull the mind to things that will gratify the senses. Silencing the pull of the mind and senses allows one's true self to emerge and be realized. The false ego, created by experiences, desires, programming and conditioning, is caused by identification with the physical body. The human form of life is meant for purification of consciousness. This is the way to Self-Realization and conscious Awareness of and communion with God, bringing the individual will into alignment with God's will, thus merging any remaining remnant of a separate will with the Supreme Will and Consciousness of God. When you accomplish this by your effort and the grace of God, you fulfill the purpose of life and return to the innocence and purity of your original Spiritual Consciousness, while still in a physical body in the material world.

Transform your consciousness from material to spiritual and go back home to the spiritual world. Everyone is meant to act under the guidance and direction of God. Man was not meant to serve his personal ego. Man is meant to serve God. We were designed to be intuitively impelled, to be guided from within. The extent of one's free will is limited to where one focuses one's attention, within or without. We have the choice to respond to either the inner wisdom of the higher self or to the conditioned responses of mental and emotional programming, traumas, conditioned patterns of thinking, feeling, willing and acting. When we are tuned in within, we are turned off to the material world. Self-reliance is depending on the guidance of God from within. Depending on what comes from within is living in Grace. A pure devotee of God does not act on his or her own account, but waits and acts under the direction of God. *"If you become conscious of Me, you will pass over all the obstacles of conditioned life by My grace. If, however, you do not work in such consciousness but act through false ego, not hearing Me, you will be lost,"* says Lord Krishna to his friend and devotee Arjuna on the battlefield of Kurukshetra ("Bhagavad-Gita As It Is," Chapter 18, Text 58).

Just as there is an administrative hierarchy in the material world, there exists an administrative hierarchy in the spiritual world to advance the plan of Man's Redemption and Awakening to his spiritual identity. There are those who oppose this hierarchy and attempt to interfere with the plan. They are the demons of mythology and the world's religions. The material creation is an organized program that provides a means for conditioned souls to have experiences that will expand their consciousness. This means that opposition is necessary as a catalyst to propel the forward movement of consciousness expansion. Spirit knows itself as the result of experience supplied by an opposing force. Duality is the nature of the material world. Because of this and the nature of a free will universe, there exists negative, aberrant and perverse expressions of consciousness. The original catastrophe mixing Man's spirit with animals let loose a Pandora's box of all kinds of expressions of consciousness that manifest themselves in the material world. Anything that inhibits spiritual growth is the only true definition of evil. Evil goes against the forward movement of expanding consciousness. A dual spirit evolution is occurring simultaneously: one, ascending; the other, descending. There are souls that are advancing spiritually, and there are souls that are receding deeper into material consciousness to de-evolve into animals. The demons wish to make this planet a closed system where it cannot function for the purpose it was intended. The material world gives Man and Woman the opportunity to purify themselves of their material consciousness, for the aim of life is to go back home to the spiritual world, back to God. **The ultimate goal of psychological warfare is to entangle mankind in materialism so that no one can return home, back to God.**

"Little children, it is the last time: and as ye have heard that antichrist shall come, even now are there many antichrists; whereby we know that it is the last time." (First Epistle of John, Chapter 2, verse 18) The idea of antichrist is that there is an individual, the antithesis of Christ, who will impersonate Christ, persuading multitudes to turn away from the mission of Christ and the Plan of Salvation to awaken Man to his spiritual identity and consciousness. The demons oppose this Awakening. They are strictly materialistic. They consider ego gratification the epitome of self-expression. Being negative entities, they feed off the negative emotions of fear, anger, hatred, envy, resentment, etc. Their individuality is an illusion manufactured by the conditioned mind to perpetuate and sustain itself in a "virtual reality" of its own making. All mental disorders are ego disorders, because of the ego's propensity to live in a make-believe world. Suffering is the result. The spirit of the beast is self-serving sense gratification, an intensification and magnification of animal instincts centered around the activities of sleeping,

eating, mating and defending, based on preserving the physical body to enjoy it rather than to transcend it. The way to extinguish the desire for individuality separate from God is by absorbing one's self in the higher self to know and experience a higher individuality where there is no tendency or inclination other than to serve God and await His direction. The Battle of Armageddon is really a conflict between two types of consciousness: material versus spiritual. The demonic, slaves to the bodily conception of life, are adverse to liberation from material bondage. Let evil know its error and come into the Light and eternal life, for all souls are sacred, being individual units of the Supreme Consciousness and meant to know the bliss of unity with that consciousness, which is not a negation of one's individuality but a realization and celebration of it as Sons and Daughters of God.

According to the Bible, the Antichrist is to appear before Christ, but what if the order of things have been switched around to make it appear that Christ is the Antichrist and vice versa? The priesthood often collaborated with the political authorities to control and exploit the people for material gain. The two were often the same. Could it be possible that people have been programmed to reject Christ and His message? Movies and television have programmed the public to respond in particular ways not only to different words, images and ideas, but also to different vocal qualities, facial expressions, body movements and gestures. The deep, resonating voice of Darth Vader in *Star Wars* is programmed as evil, but it is also a voice that personifies authority. The wide-eyed stare of zombies, the insane and the violent is programmed as evil, but a child looks at the world with the wide-eyed stare of innocence. Extreme mood changes from laughter to crying is normal behavior for children, but this same behavior exhibited by adults is called "mental illness." Our voices, faces and bodies are capable of a far greater range of expression than is actually displayed because we have been programmed to be "human". Man is part animal, human and divine. The ultimate conspiracy is to keep Man human, while Man is on the upward climb to return to his original, divine Consciousness. *"Therefore if any man be in Christ, he is a new creature: old things are passed away; behold, all things are become new."* (2 Corinthians 5:17)

"I see no obvious impediments to humans giving rise to another species, one that is still more highly evolved," says paleontologist Dale Russell of the Canadian National Museum of Natural Sciences.[271] Scientists

91

believe that man is evolving.[272] The fossil record shows that large-scale transformations can happen abruptly.[273] Man approaches evolutionary change and the appearance of the New Man. "The most awesome and profound knowledge awaits us," says James Westphal, professor of planetary sciences at the California Institute of Technology, "and the most exciting will be those things we just haven't dreamed about yet."[274]

The material world is a dream world where relationships are not what they seem. The most perplexing relationship for men and women is the relationship between men and women. The doctrine of Original Sin centers around sex. Man was not always as he is today in physical form. Spirit as spirit can take on any form as a vehicle for expression and learning. The dual nature of man and woman, separate now, was once one. *"So God created man in his own image, in the image of God created he him; male and female created he them."* (Genesis 1:27) *"And the Lord God said, It is not good that the man should be alone; I will make him an help meet for him."* (Genesis 2:18) Man was originally androgynous – male and female combined, first in spirit, then in a single biological organism that evolved into two separate and distinct sexes. *"For man is not of the woman; but the woman is of the man."* (I Corinthians 11:8) The story of the creation of Eve is symbolic of the dividing of the sexes where woman was taken out of, subtracted from man. *"And Adam said, This is now bone of my bones, and flesh of my flesh: she shall be called woman, because she was taken out of man."* (Genesis 2:23) The deep sleep that fell upon Adam and the creation of Eve from Adam's rib is symbolic of the gradual evolution and separation of the sexes, which was followed by the development and growth of civilization.

"If we appear in outward form and mind

A various, degraded, motley kind,

Wonder no more – the cause is all too plain;

We've mixed and changed ourselves – must change again."

- the Greek poet Theognes

6th Century BC

Originally, man and woman were one. Consciousness split and divided into masculine and feminine in two distinct and separate physical bodies. Woman was a subtraction of qualities and traits from man so that both might know the other by contrast and thus gain greater awareness of themselves. Man and woman embody the missing half of one another's total nature. In separation, man longs for the woman he separated from and woman longs for the man she separated from to be complete. The desire for union between man and woman is in reality the desire to re-unite with whom one was separated from and balance masculine and feminine qualities and traits within one's own self. The purpose of having children is to educate and deliver them from the suffering of the material world and break the cycle of repeated birth and death so that they may return home to the spiritual world. It is the destiny of man and woman to achieve completion through the union of opposites within his and her own body. Such a state of balance and equilibrium was achieved by Jeshua (Jesus) as Christ, resulting in the demonstration of extraordinary super-human powers which are a natural outcome of total and complete absorption in God Consciousness. Let society be organized and administered for the spiritual emancipation of mankind from the bondage of material consciousness.

MIND CONTROL IS BEING USED ON AN UNSUSPECTING PUBLIC. MIND CONTROL IS BEING USED ON AN UNSUSPECTING PUBLIC.
MIND CONTROL IS BEING USED ON AN UNSUSPECTING PUBLIC. MIND CONTROL IS BEING USED ON AN UNSUSPECTING PUBLIC.
MIND CONTROL IS BEING USED ON AN UNSUSPECTING PUBLIC. MIND CONTROL IS BEING USED ON AN UNSUSPECTING PUBLIC.
MIND CONTROL IS BEING USED ON AN UNSUSPECTING PUBLIC. MIND CONTROL IS BEING USED ON AN UNSUSPECTING PUBLIC.
MIND CONTROL IS BEING USED ON AN UNSUSPECTING PUBLIC. MIND CONTROL IS BEING USED ON AN UNSUSPECTING PUBLIC.
MIND CONTROL IS BEING USED ON AN UNS   ING USED ON AN UNSUSPECTING PUBLIC.
MIND CONTROL IS BEING USED ON AN UN   ING USED ON AN UNSUSPECTING PUBLIC.

SECTION 24
Postscript

MIND CONTROL IS BEING USED ON AN U   ING USED ON AN UNSUSPECTING PUBLIC.
MIND CONTROL IS BEING USED ON AN U   ING USED ON AN UNSUSPECTING PUBLIC.
MIND CONTROL IS BEING USED ON AN U   ING USED ON AN UNSUSPECTING PUBLIC.
MIND CONTROL IS BEING USED ON AN U   ING USED ON AN UNSUSPECTING PUBLIC.
MIND CONTROL IS BEING USED ON AN U   ING USED ON AN UNSUSPECTING PUBLIC.
MIND CONTROL IS BEING USED ON AN UNSUSPECTING PUBLIC. MIND CONTROL IS BEING USED ON AN UNSUSPECTING PUBLIC.
MIND CONTROL IS BEING USED ON AN UNSUSPECTING PUBLIC. MIND CONTROL IS BEING USED ON AN UNSUSPECTING PUBLIC.
MIND CONTROL IS BEING USED ON AN UNSUSPECTING PUBLIC. MIND CONTROL IS BEING USED ON AN UNSUSPECTING PUBLIC.
MIND CONTROL IS BEING USED ON AN UNSUSPECTING PUBLIC. MIND CONTROL IS BEING USED ON AN UNSUSPECTING PUBLIC.
MIND CONTROL IS BEING USED ON AN UNSUSPECTING PUBLIC. MIND CONTROL IS BEING USED ON AN UNSUSPECTING PUBLIC.
MIND CONTROL IS BEING USED ON AN UNSUSPECTING PUBLIC. MIND CONTROL IS BEING USED ON AN UNSUSPECTING PUBLIC.

As far back as I can remember, I had a longing and compelling need to truly understand what was *really* going on here even as a child. It was years later when I had somewhat of an education and a vocabulary that I realized that what I was feeling at five was existential "angst" (anxiety). Try to imagine that for a five year old. I did not understand why I found Life to be as it is. The question I asked myself early in public school and continued to ask through college was: "How do I know that what they are telling me is true?" This question applied not only to education but also to the media and society's other institutions including organized religion. "How do I know that what they are telling me is true?" The answer was: "I don't know." The only way to truly know anything is by direct experience and direct observation unencumbered by preconceived notions. But we humans have a tendency and a history of making mistakes and perceiving things incorrectly. And so there must be a higher standard by which to know the Truth. Until knowing what that was, I had no choice other than to be open to consider anything and everything, all points of view and to be non-judgmental, simply because I did not know what the purpose of Life was and how it was to be attained, but I had a child's faith in God that one day all would be revealed.

In 1980, I was given the results of private research investigating mental programming, deprogramming and reprogramming. My father was a hypnotist, researcher and consultant to the medical profession for more than 20 years. As a hypnotist he used language to create sounds by varying inflection and pacing to guide the listener through deeper, more relaxed levels of body and mind. He would often say, "Good health begins in the mind," which makes perfect sense since whatever is going on in the mind will manifest in the physical body. Negative thoughts and emotions will affect mental and physical health just as positive thoughts and emotions will, especially with repetition over time. His research led to the development of a unique audio titled "Personal Comfort Training" that helps the listener identify deeper, more relaxed levels of mind in order to enter them at will and function in them for extended periods of time. The verbal message is a health program that speaks directly to the subconscious. His turning over his research to me in 1980 led me to leave the career I was pursuing to research the issue of mind control. I was working as a film editor in New York City at the time. I studied film at the Boston University School of Communications and worked in the film industry for 13 years. As a film editor I saw how simple it is to change the meaning of an event or of what someone says through editing. I was aware of how plastic and moldable mass media reality is, but I did not fully appreciate the extent to which we are all manipulated and controlled by mass media (even those who work in it) until my father gave me his research and I began to work with it, discovering that mind control is being used on an unsuspecting public.

Along with the research and audios, my father gave me a copy of *The Golden Scripts* transcribed by William Dudley Pelley and the twelve-volume *Soulcraft Scripts* and other books of the Soulcraft Teaching. Someone had given my father several other books that he thought I would be interested in. One was Gary Allen's *None Dare Call It Conspiracy* and the other, Peter McAlpine's *The Occult Technology of Power*, both about the "conspiracy theory" of history. It was time for me to accept the responsibility to educate myself and get what I needed and did not get from public school and college. I started with the bibliography at the end of these two books and began to investigate alternative sources of information to see what was available on a variety of topics, including history, politics, economics, psychology, religion. The book *Mind Control in the United States*, published in 1985, was the result, followed by the audio presentation *Mind Control in America* in 1991, *Wake-Up America* in 1995 and the revised and updated edition of *Mind Control in the United States* published in 2015. I was interviewed on numerous radio talk shows for about a dozen years, when I stopped to focus on my spiritual practice and study. My mother was my biggest fan and supporter. A mother is a child's first spiritual teacher by example. She passed in 2007 at the age of 85, six months after the passing of my father in 2006 at the age of 88. She gave me the poem "If" by Rudyard Kipling when I was a young man. A copy appears in the Appendix B. May it inspire and guide you or someone you know as it has done for me.

A major problem in the world is the unwillingness of so many people to put themselves in the shoes of their neighbor and view things as someone else may see them. This is particularly true when it comes to religion. People tend to believe that the religion they were born into is the best of all religions. This attitude of exclusivity and superiority where one believes that his or her race, religion and culture is the only one that has any validity is divisive and prevents true understanding. Those who are mature in spiritual insight recognize and respect the universal truth contained in all races, religions and cultures and not just the one they happened to be born into. No nation and no people have an exclusive monopoly on the truth. Truth has been deposited among the many peoples of the world, representing different angles of vision that reveal a wider view and greater understanding when taken into account. There is only one race, the human race and its subdivisions that manifest in a variety of forms. There are things that all people share in common regardless of race and religion. We are all born into this world, we stay for a short time and then the body dies. A problem arises when, due to material consciousness, people misidentify themselves as the physical body, mind and ego-personality. One's true identity is spirit-soul, an individual unit of God's Consciousness, experiencing Life as a human being in a variety of shapes, sizes, colors, heights, weights, environments, conditions and circumstances with the high purpose of the spiritual emancipation of mankind from the limitations and bondage of material consciousness. There can be only one religion, the essence of which is to love and serve God, to love one another, to love thy neighbor as thyself, to love thy enemy, to forgive, to have mercy and compassion for one another, to honor the divinity that resides within all mankind and all living beings, to give no creature cause to fear you, to go to the aid of all in need of help under the guidance and direction of God. This is how Man manifests and expresses his divinity and oneness with God. Love is the key to all knowledge, wisdom and power. Love is the only true religion.

Teach your children the truth and they will fulfill the purpose of life and lead the way to a New Age of spirituality. It is important that the child growing up in poverty in an urban ghetto or rural countryside or the child growing up in affluence in a mansion or in a palace and all in between know the purpose of life and how to attain it. It is the birthright of all children. It is one of the ironies of life that those who are materially poor are in a better position to advance spiritually than their wealthy brethren. Wealth is a temptation and a snare that entraps the unwary and unmindful. It is for this reason that Yeshua (Jesus) said: "It is easier for a camel to go through the eye of a needle than for a rich man to enter the kingdom of God." (Mark 10:25) Young and old alike are taught that only money and material things matter in life and this misconception must be exposed as the great lie that it is. Wealth can be both a blessing and a curse. Wealth affords both resources and leisure that are best used in advancing the program to educate the world about the necessity for God Consciousness as the only solution for the problems and suffering of material existence.

The world does not operate in the way that many people think it does. Government does not operate as many people think. The banks do not operate as many people think. In fact, most things do not operate in the way people think.

There are more things in Heaven and Earth, Horatio,

than are dreamt of in your philosophy.

-William Shakespeare

Hamlet, Act 1, Scene 5

We must heal our nation and world by healing the hearts and minds of mankind. For there to be a change in how people treat one another, there must be a change within people first – a change in consciousness. Inner change brings about outward change, and change occurs as the result of something happening: an event or series of events or revelations of new information that changes how people view the world and themselves.

The United States of America has a special destiny to fulfill because this nation is comprised of people of varied backgrounds, races, cultures and religions from around the world. America is more than a nation. It is an ideal, an aspiration for the highest good for all mankind. We, as a nation, must live up to that ideal and aspiration. We must acknowledge and heal the deep wounds caused by slavery and racism and make amends for it and help black people who continue to suffer because of it. We must help native Americans who were dispossessed of their lands, their culture and population decimated. We must help all who cry out in distress for aid and comfort: the poor, the destitute, the homeless, all who are in need of help for that is what true family does and we are all members of that family. There is enough for everyone. There is no need for lack. It is due to gross mismanagement and greed. Society is not being administered for the highest good of all people equally.

We must put an end to a dishonest money system that enriches a few at the expense of the many and the idea that there are institutions too big to fail and men and women too powerful to go to prison for their crimes against humanity. There exists a criminal syndicate at the very pinnacle of power that is sucking the life out of this nation and planet. An Anglo-American-Zionist alliance seeks to transform America and the world through the Hegelian dialectic of crisis creation and management into a totalitarian dictatorship: the New World Order. This situation has developed because the fundamental, core problem for mankind is that people do not know who and what they really are nor the purpose of life and how to attain it and thus are subject to all manner of deception and manipulation, getting caught and stuck in a world of illusion. Spiritual practice is meant to break through that illusion so that one awakens to who and what one really is as a direct experience, felt fully and completely where true understanding is realized within as Pure Awareness prior to and beyond the body and mind.

> "Know ye not that ye are the temple of God and that the Spirit of God dwelleth in you." (1 Corinthians 3:16)

> "I have said, Ye are gods; and all of you are children of the most High." (Psalm 82:6)

> ". . . the kingdom of God is within you." (Luke 17:21)

All spiritual work is directed towards purification of consciousness and dissolving the false-ego and its programming. The objective is to disappear this false identity in order to realize by direct experience one's true spiritual nature as Pure Being, Pure Consciousness, Pure Awareness, Pure Spirit. This is the simple truth about spiritual practice. In actuality, it is a rigorous discipline requiring sincerity of purpose, time, effort, perseverance and, above all, faith in God.

"I AM the place where God shines through,

For God and Man are one not two.

I need not fear, not fret, nor plan.

God needs and wants me as I AM.

So if I'll be relaxed and free,

He'll manifest Himself through me."[275]

APPENDIX - A

TV: THE MOST POWERFUL PSYCHOLOGICAL WARFARE WEAPON

Television is the most powerful weapon of psychological warfare in history. This fact is so important it bears repeating: Television is the most powerful weapon of psychological warfare in history.

Most people do not think of their televisions as weapons because they are regarded as members of the family in many households across the country. Television has been entrusted with the care of the youth of this nation as a baby sitter. For many people, it is the primary source of news, information and entertainment. After a hard day of life in America, many people come home tired and plop themselves down on the sofa or their favorite easy chair, reach for the remote, turn on the TV and put their mind on hold.

Think of the times you have observed young children or senior citizens motionless in front of the TV. They wear a vacant, glassy-eyed look on their faces because they are in a trance-like state. Although it is not consciously perceived, the picture projected on the TV screen is actually flickering. We do not see the flickering consciously, but subconsciously the repetitive pattern of the flickering image induces a hypnotic state of mind in those who are vulnerable to that form of psychological suggestion.

Since television is literally "plugging" itself into the brain and central nervous system, our bodies are physiologically, as well as psychologically, responding to television.

Though there are an innumerable progression of examples, one stands out as memorable to many. In December, 1997, 700 children in Japan were hospitalized after watching an episode of the popular "Pokémon" TV cartoon. On this particular episode, stroboscopic flashes of light pulsated from the eyes of one of the cartoon's characters, causing epileptic-like seizures in some of the children who were viewing it. Other children experienced muscle spasms, dizziness and nausea.

Attention deficit disorder was practically unheard of before the advent of television. Constantly changing camera angles and quick cutting from one scene to another, techniques that were developed for TV commercials and music videos, have been more common among the various types of programming. These techniques effectively train into the brain a short attention span for the beholder. Programs edited in this manner cause corresponding electro-chemical changes in the brain which releases endorphins to cause viewers to experience a drug-like effect.

A child sitting motionless while fixated on the TV screen is getting an electronic "fix." Children who are fidgety, unable to focus and demonstrating nervous energy will often calm down quickly when allowed to sit and watch TV. This scenario infers that children can become psychologically and physiologically-addicted to television in a manner every bit as serious as an addiction to drugs, alcohol or cigarettes.

The principles of mind control, hypnotic suggestion and mental programming are ancient. Modern technology allows the implementation of these age-old principles on a scale massive enough to influence the thinking and behavior of large numbers of people. The goal of those using modern technology to program the thoughts and actions of entire nations is to suspend the thought processes of the conscious mind and leave them open to suggestion.

The first objective of the commercial advertiser or the government propagandist is to create the conditions that will produce a state of mind favorable to receiving their message(s). That state of mind is the hypnotic state and television is capable of inducing this altered state of consciousness automatically, regardless of program content, due to the nature of the medium itself.

This makes television the most potent instrument of mass persuasion in the history of the world.

Think for a moment about the way newscasters speak and you will realize that they all talk the same way regardless of ethnic background. Whether they are black, white, hispanic or oriental, with few exceptions, they all sound alike. The patterned speech of the newscaster is similar to that of a hypnotist. The newscaster looks directly into the camera and into the eyes of the viewer—a technique that has been used by hypnotists for centuries.

Coupled with the newscaster being a trusted and respected authority figure, his ability to encourage acceptance of the information being presented as true and accurate is magnified.

It is no accident that television networks have "programming" departments, that the lineup of shows is called "programming" and each individual show is called a "program." The Orwellian world of mind control is a present day reality. It arrived unnoticed because people were conditioned not to notice. There could be no effective propaganda without the support of the mass media in general and television in particular.

The consolidation of the ownership of presses, radio, television and movies makes the coordination of propaganda possible. Though generally regarded as a classic work of fiction, the novel "1984" by George Orwell was a warning of what would happen to people who lost their freedom of mind without being "aware" while it was being taken from them through artful abuses of emotional and intellectual mind manipulation/control techniques.

Most people do not pay conscious attention to things that affect them subconsciously. They do not usually know what to look for until these things are pointed out to them. The most effective way to protect yourself, your family and your community from subconscious manipulation is by being aware of how it works.

According to Homer Simpson, the underachieving father figure on the long-running adult cartoon "The Simpsons," the answers to life's problems are on TV. And, like cartoon characters, the American people have been programmed to turn on the TV and select network programming for answers.

Our world has devolved to a state of perpetual war and conflict. That the people tolerate this state is due largely to psychological warfare being waged on them through television programming. This places mind control at the top of the list as the most important issue facing society today.

Ask yourself, if the people were in control of their own thoughts and not influenced by a barrage of media-induced propaganda, would they, on their own authority, tolerate the world as it exists today or would they demand a more just, compassionate and cooperative world?

The first freedom from which all other freedoms are derived is freedom of the mind. If the present state of world affairs is to change, we will have to break free of the programming and begin thinking independently again.

APPENDIX - B

If—

If you can keep your head when all about you
    Are losing theirs and blaming it on you,
If you can trust yourself when all men doubt you,
    But make allowance for their doubting too;
If you can wait and not be tired by waiting,
    Or being lied about, don't deal in lies,
Or being hated, don't give way to hating,
    And yet don't look too good, nor talk too wise:

If you can dream—and not make dreams your master;
    If you can think—and not make thoughts your aim;
If you can meet with Triumph and Disaster
    And treat those two impostors just the same;
If you can bear to hear the truth you've spoken
    Twisted by knaves to make a trap for fools,
Or watch the things you gave your life to, broken,
    And stoop and build 'em up with worn-out tools:

If you can make one heap of all your winnings
    And risk it on one turn of pitch-and-toss,
And lose, and start again at your beginnings
    And never breathe a word about your loss;
If you can force your heart and nerve and sinew
    To serve your turn long after they are gone,
And so hold on when there is nothing in you
    Except the Will which says to them: 'Hold on!'

If you can talk with crowds and keep your virtue,
    Or walk with Kings—nor lose the common touch,
If neither foes nor loving friends can hurt you,
    If all men count with you, but none too much;
If you can fill the unforgiving minute
    With sixty seconds' worth of distance run,
Yours is the Earth and everything that's in it,
    And—which is more—you'll be a Man, my son!

- Rudyard Kipling (1865 - 1936)

BENEDICTION

"The Lord bless thee, and keep thee:

The Lord make His face shine upon thee,
and be gracious unto thee:

The Lord lift up His countenance upon thee,
and give thee peace."

- Numbers 6:24-26

FOOTNOTES

1 Faber Birren, *Color & Human Response*, (New York: Van Nostrand Reinhold Company, 1978), p. 69.
2 Norman F. Dixon, *Subliminal Perception: The Nature of a Controversy*, (London: McGraw-Hill, 1971), p. 303.
3 Steven Halpern, Ph.D., *Tuning The Human Instrument*, (Belmont, Calif.: Spectrum Research Institute, 1978), p. 47.
4 *Life*, October 3, 1969, p. 74.
5 Salem Kirban, "Rock Music Is Big Business," in *Satan's Music Exposed* by Lowell Hart, (Huntington Valley, Pa.: Salem Kirban, 1981), p. 45.
6 Paul Haack, "Is Big Brother Watching?" *Music Educators Journal*, May, 1982, p. 26.
7 Wilson Bryan Key, *Subliminal Seduction*, (Englewood Cliffs: Prentice-Hall, 1973), pp. 91-92.
8 Jacob Aranza, *Backward Masking Unmasked*, (Shreveport, La.: Huntington House, 1983), pp. 1-2. Also, N. F. Dixon, *Subliminal Perception*, pp. 53-54.
9 Aranza, *Backward Masking Unmasked*, p. 6.
10 Wilson Bryan Key, *Media Sexploitation*, (Englewood Cliffs: Prentice-Hall, 1976), p. 120.
11 Ibid., p. 118.
12 Lynn E. Moller, "Music in Germany During the Third Reich: The Use of Music for Propaganda," Music Educators Journal, November, 1980, p. 40.
13 Haack, "Is Big Brother Watching?" p. 27.
14 Dick Sutphen, *Unseen Influences*, (New York: Pocket Books, 1982), p. 28.
15 Key, *Subliminal Seduction*, p. 135.
16 Marya Mannes, "Ain't Nobody Here But Us Commercials," *Reporter*, October 17, 1957, p. 35.
17 Dixon, *Subliminal Perception*.
18 Olivia Goodkin and Maureen Ann Phillips, "The Subconscious Taken Captive: A Social, Ethical, and Legal Analysis of Subliminal Communication Technology," *Southern California Law Review*, July, 1980, p. 1081.
19 "TV's 'Invisible Ads' Called Ineffective," *Science Digest*, May, 1958. pp. 22-23.
20 Wilson Bryan Key, *The Clam-Plate Orgy: And Other Subliminal Techniques for Manipulating Your Behavior*, (Englewood Cliffs: Prentice-Hall, 1980), p.148.
21 *Science Digest*, May, 1958, p. 23.
22 Herbert Brean, "Hidden Sell Technique Is Almost Here," *Life*, March 31, 1958, pp. 102-104+.
23 Key, Media Sexploitation, p. 116.
24 "50 Stores Use Subliminal Messages, Expert Says,(UPI)," *Winston-Salem Journal*, August 8, 1984, p. 13.
25 Stimutech, Inc., 16262 Chandler Road, East Lansing, Michigan, 48823.
26 Brean, *Hidden Sell Technique Is Almost Here*.
27 Key, *Media Sexploitation*, pp. 102-103.
28 Ibid., p. 112.

29 Ibid., p. 111.
30 Ibid., p. 110
31 Ibid., p. 99.
32 Goodkin and Phillips, "The Subconscious Taken Captive" p. 1084 citing Lee, "The CIA's Subliminal Seduction," *High Times*, February, 1980, p. 96.
33 Ibid., p. 1084.
34 Raymond Fielding, *The American Newsreel* 1911-1967, (Norman: University of Oklahoma Press, 1972), p. 241.
35 Thomson Jay Hudson, Ph.D., LL.D., *The Law of Psychic Phenomena*, (New York: Samuel Weiser, 1968), p. 30.
36 Ibid., pp. 151-152.
37 Ibid., p. 87.
38 Harry Arons, *The New Master Course In Hypnotism*, (Irvington, New Jersey: Powers Publishers, 1961), p. 31.
39 Howard S. Becker, *Outsiders,* (New York: The Free Press, 1963), pp. 135-146.
40 "Marihuana: New Federal Tax Hits Dealings in Potent Weed," *Newsweek*, August 14, 1937, Science Section.
41 Lester Grinspoon, M.D., *Marihuana Reconsidered*, (Cambridge: Harvard University Press, 1971), p. 26.
42 Jacques Ellul, *Propaganda: the Formation of Men's Attitudes*, Translated by Konrad Kellen and Jean Lerner, (New York: Alfred A. Knopf, 1965), p. 27.
43 Ibid., p. 132.
44 Grinspoon, *Marihuana Reconsidered*, p. 301.
45 Ibid., p. 236.
46 Ibid., p. 241.
47 Ibid., p. 24.
48 Becker, *Outsiders*, pp. 141-142.
49 E. Merrill Root, *Brainwashing in the High Schools*, (New York: The Devin-Adair Company, 1958), p. 15.
50 Ibid., p. 28.
51 Ibid., p. 29.
52 Ibid., pp. 41 & 99.
53 Ibid., p. 13.
54 Jonathan L. Freedman, *Introductory Psychology*, (second edition), (Reading, Mass.: Addison-Wesley Publishing Co., 1982), p. 285.
55 Hudson, *Law of Psychic Phenomena*, p. 87.
56 Freedman, *Introductory Psychology*, p. 291.
57 Margaret O. Hyde, *Brainwashing and Other Forms of Mind Control*, (New York: McGraw-Hill Book Company, 1977), pp. 92-93.
58 Denise Winn, *The Manipulated Mind: Brainwashing, Conditioning and Indoctrination*, (London: The Octagon Press, 1983), p. 148.
59 Ibid., p. 148.
60 *The Occult Technology of Power: A Project of the Society for Illuminating the Sources of Power*, (Dearborn, Michigan: Alpine Enterprises, 1974), pp. 45-47.
61 Ibid., pp. 530-531.

62 Dixon, *Subliminal Perception*, p. 3.
63 *The Occult Technology of Power*, p. 31.
64 Ellul, *Propaganda*, p. 13.
65 Ibid., p. vi.
66 Ibid., p. vi & 111.
67 Leonard Louis Levinson, *Bartlett's Unfamiliar Quotations*, (Chicago: Cowles Book Co., Inc. 1971), p. 203.
68 Jane E. Brody, N.Y. Times News Service, Some Experts Doubt the Power of Subliminal Messages, *Winston-Salem Journal*, August 22, 1982, p. C3.
69 Key, *Subliminal Seduction*, p. 189.
70 Key, *Subliminal Seduction, Media Sexploitation, and The Clam Plate Orgy.*
71 *Donna Woolfolk Cross, Media-Speak*, (New York: New American Library, 1983), p. 46 citing Advertising Age, July 19, 1965, p. 42.
72 Ibid., p. 45.
73 Key, *The Clam-Plate Orgy*, p. 148.
74 Key, *Media Sexploitation*, p. 167.
75 Robert Reginald and James Natal, "George Orwell's 1984—How Close Are We?" in *The People's Almanac #2*, David Wallechinsky and Irving Wallace, (New York: Bantam Books, 1978), pp. 54-55.
76 "State Department Strikes 'Killing' From Reports," *Winston-Salem Journal*, February 11, 1984, p. 14.
77 Norman Podhoretz, "1984 Is Here: Where Is Big Brother?" *Reader's Digest*, January, 1984, p. 33.
78 Edwin M. Yoder, Jr., Washington Post Writers Group, "1984—Fantasy Year Could Never Be Otherwise," *The Sentinel*, December 10, 1983, p. 10.
79 Cross, *Media-Speak*, p. 42 citing Arthur Asa Berger, "The TV-Guided American," p. 5.
80 John Bartlett, *Familiar Quotations*, (Boston: Little Brown & Co., 1937), p. 370 citing *The American Crisis*, No. IV, September 12, 1777.
81 Carl J. Friedrich and Zbigniew K. Brzezinski, *Totalitarian Dictatorship and Autocracy*, (Cambridge: Harvard University Press, 1965), p. 129.
82 Ellul, *Propaganda*, p. 102.
83 83 Ibid., p. 103.
84 Benjamin M. Compaine, ed., *Who Owns The Media: Concentration of Ownership in the Mass Communications Industry*, (White Plains, New York: Knowledge Industry Publications, Inc., 1979), p. 179.
85 Ibid., p. 190.
86 Ibid., p. 191.
87 Mort Rosenblum, Associated Press, "When in Rome, Do as Americans Do: Order a Big Mac," *Winston-Salem Journal*, March 4, 1984, p. C1.
88 Ibid., p. C1.
89 Richard Gertner, ed., *International Motion Picture Almanac*, 1979 edition, (New York: Quigley Publishing Co., Inc.), p. 491.
90 *Who's Who in America*, Volume 36, 1970-1971, (Chicago: Marquis Who's Who, Inc.), p. 1932. Also, *International Motion Picture Almanac*, 1979 edition, p. 491.

91 Richard Gertner, ed., *International Motion Picture Almanac*, 1983 edition, p. 482. *Financial information from Moody's Investors Fact Sheets*, Vol. 4, No. 49, Sec. 50, File N8401, June 18, 1981. "Walter Scott's Personality Parade", *Parade Magazine*, January 20, 1985, p. 2.

92 Gary Deeb, Field Newspaper Syndicate, "ABC Apparently Is Dazzled by Kissinger," *Winston-Salem Journal*, October 9, 1982.

93 Richard Gertner, ed., *International Motion Picture Almanac*, 1982 edition, p. 452.

94 Standard & Poor's Register of Corporations, *Directors and Executives*, (New York: Standard & Poor's Corp., 1984), Vol. 1, p. 1565.

95 William Murphy, "World War II Propaganda Films," *Propaganda—The Art of Persuasion: World War II*, Anthony Rhodes, (New York: Chelsea House Publishers, 1976).

96 Dwight Macdonald, Einstein, Pudovkin and Others, *The Emergence of Film Art*, Lewis Jacobs, (New York: Hopkinson and Blake, Publishers, 1969), p. 122.

97 Ellul, *Propaganda*, p. 68.

98 Fred Silva, ed., *Focus on The Birth of a Nation*, (Englewood Cliffs: Prentice-Hall, 1971), pp. 1-15.

99 "A Street-Gang Movie Called 'The Warriors' Triggers A Puzzling, Tragic Wave of Audience Violence and Death," *People*, March 12, 1979, pp. 37-38. Also, N.Y. Times Index, 1979, p. 831.

100 Peter Koper, "Can Movies Kill?" *American Film*, July-August 1982, pp. 46-51.

101 James Mann, "What Is TV Doing To America?" *U.S. News and World Report*, August 2, 1982, p. 27.

102 Harry F. Waters, Nancy Stadtman, and Chuck Twardy, "Fallout Over "The Day After,'" *Newsweek*, October 24, 1983, p. 126.

103 "Callers 'So Glad It's Just a Movie,'" Associated Press, *The Sentinel*, April 30, 1984, p. 15.

104 Perry London, *Behavior Control*, (New York: Harper & Row, Publishers, 1971), p. 4.

105 Ibid., pp. 76-77.

106 Ibid., p. 77.

107 Desmond Morris, Peter Collett, Peter Marsh and Marie O'Shaugnessy, *Gestures: Their Origin and Distribution*, (New York: Stein and Day Publishers, 1979) p. xi.

108 Julius Fast, *Body Language*, (New York: M. Evans and Co., Inc., 1970), p. 129.

109 Ibid., p. 182.

110 G. William Domhoff, *The Powers That Be: Processes of Ruling Class Domination in America*, (New York: Random House, 1978), pp. 136-137.

111 "Roger Mudd Criticized," Associated Press, Winston-Salem Journal March 15, 1984, p. 32.

112 David Wallechinsky and Irving Wallace, *The Peoples' Almanac #3*, (New York: Bantam Books, 1981), p. 132.

113 Rose K. Goldsen, *The Show and Tell Machine*, (New York: Dell Publishing Company, 1977), pp. 65-72.

114 Bob Green, "An Early Encounter With Gary Hart," *Chicago Tribune Syndicate*, Winston-Salem Journal, March 21, 1984, p.. 4.

115 Gary Allen, *None Dare Call It Conspiracy*, (Rossmoor, Calif.: Concord Press, 1971), p. 23.

116 Ibid., p. 24.

117 W. Cleon Skousen, *The Naked Capitalist*, (Salt Lake City, Utah: author's private edition, 1970), p. 7.

118 Ibid., p. 22.

119 Ferdinand Lundberg, *America's 60 Families*, (New York: The Vanguard Press, 1937), p. 3.

120 Ibid., pp. 8-9. Also, Domhoff, *The Powers That Be*, p. 20 citing Philip H. Buruch, Jr., "The Managerial Revolution Reassessed," (Heath-Lexington, 1972).

121 Lundberg, *America's 60 Famili*es, p. 50.

122 Ibid., p. 50.

123 Ibid., p. 53.

124 *The Occult Technology of Power*, p. 7.

125 Edward Bellamy, *Equality*, (New York: D. Appleton and Co., 1897. Republished by Scholarly Press, Grosse Pointe, Mich.), pp. 195-200.

126 Dr. Carroll Quigley, *Tragedy and Hope—A History of the World In Our Time*, (New York: The Macmillan Company, 1966), p. 950.

127 Wallechinsky and Wallace, *The People's Almanac # 3*, p. 253. Also, G. William Domhoff, *Who Rules America?* (Englewood Cliffs: Prenctice-Hall, Inc., 1967).

128 G. William Domhoff, *The Higher Circles: The Governing Class in America*, (New York: Random House, 1970), pp. 121-122.

129 Joseph Kraft, "School for Statesmen," *Harper's Magazine*, July, 1958, pp. 64 & 68.

130 Domhoff, *The Powers That Be*, p. 66.

131 Council on Foreign Relations, Inc., "Annual Report 1982-1983," *Membership Roster*, pp. 166-181.

132 Domhoff, *The Powers That Be*, p.67 citing Laurence H. Shoup and William Minter, *Imperial Brain Trust*, (Monthly Review Press, 1977), p. 242.

133 Allen, *None Dare Call It Conspiracy*, pp. 91-92.

134 Domhoff, *The Powers That Be*, p. 67.

135 Wallechinsky and Wallace, *The People's Almanac #3*, p. 87.

136 Ibid., pp. 87-88. Also, Michael Banovitch, "The State of Publishing: A Conspiracy,"*Critique Journal*, Fall/Winter, 1982/83, pp. 171-173.

137 Council on Foreign Relations, "Annual Report 1982-1983," p. 173.

138 Wallechinsky and Wallace, *The People's Almanac #3*, p. 87. Also, Domhoff, *Who Rules America, The Higher Circles,*" and *The Powers That Be.*

139 *Who's Who in America*, 42nd edition, 1982 - 1983, Vol. 2, p. 2832. Also, Council on Foreign Relations, Inc., "Annual Report," 1982- 1983, pp. 162-163.

140 Allen, *None Dare Call It Conspiracy*, p. 83.

141 Ibid., p. 87.

142 Ibid., pp. 79-81.

143 Ibid., pp. 92-93.

144 Ibid., p. 92.

145 Ibid., p. 129.

146 Ibid., pp. 93-95.

147 Wallechinsky and Wallace, *The People's Almanac #3*, p. 79.

148 Ibid., pp. 81-82. Walter Mondale listed as Bilderberg member on p.105 on *Trilateralism: The Trilateral Commission and Elite Planning for World Management*, edited by Holly Sklar, (Boston: South End Press, 1980).

149 Allen, *None Dare Call It Conspiracy*, p. 93.

150 Ibid., p. 70 citing *De Goulevitch, Czarism and the Revolution*, (translated from the original French publication by N. J. Couriss and reprinted by Omni Publications, Hawthorne, Calif.), 1961, pp. 223-225, 231-232.

151 Allen, *None Dare Call It Conspiracy*, p. 73.

152 Ibid., p. 59.

153 James Kunen, *The Strawberry Statement: Notes of a College Revolutionary*, (New York: Random House, 1968), p. 112.

154 Allen, *None Dare Call It Conspiracy*, pp. 121 -122.

155 Jack London, *The Iron Heel*, (New York: Grayson Publishing Corp., 1948), p. 132.

156 Ibid., p. 141.

157 Allen, *None Dare Call It Conspiracy*, p. 35.

158 Wallechinsky and Wallace, *The People's Almanac #3*, pp. 88-97.

159 *The Republic of Plato*, translated by Francis Macdonald Cornford, (London: Oxford University Press, 1973).

160 Friedrich and Brzezinski, *Totalitarian Dictatorship and Autocracy,* pp 60-69.

161 *The Republic of Plato*, pp. 67, 88-90.

162 Emanuel M. Josephson, *Rockefeller Internationalist: The Man Who Misrules The World*, (New York: Chedney Press, 1952), p. 129.

163 Frederick Eby, *The Development of Modern Education*, (Englewood Cliffs: Prenctice-Hall, 1952), p. 651.

164 Allen Johnson and Dumas Malone, ed., *Dictionary of American Biography*, Vol. VII, (New York: Charles Scribner's Sons, 1931), p. 183.

165 Josephson, *Rockefeller Internationalist*, p. 73.

166 Ellul, *Propaganda*, p. 13.

167 Ibid., p. vi.

168 Antony C. Sutton, *Western Technology and Soviet Economic Development*, Volumes 1,2,3, (Stanford, Calif.: Stanford University, Hoover Institution on War, Revolution and Peace, 1968, 1971, 1973).

169 Sutton, *Western Technology & Soviet Economic Development*, Vol. 1, p. 6.

170 Sutton, *Western Technology & Soviet Economic Development*, Vol 2, p. 3.

171 Sutton, *Western Technology & Soviet Economic Development*, Vol 3, p.383

172 Ibid., p. 381.

173 "An Eroding Dream: Percentage of Americans Owning Homes Has Fallen Since 1980," Associated Press, *Winston-Salem Journal*, May 2, 1984, p. 7.

174 "Again, The Fear of Foreclosure," *Newsweek*, January 17, 1983, p. 12.

175 James Krone, Jr., "Plowing Under the Family Farm," *The Nation*, June 2, 1979, pp. 629-630.

176 Lillian Doris, ed., *The American Way in Taxation: Internal Revenue*, 1862-1963, (Englewood Cliffs: Prentice-Hall, 1963), p. 25.

177 Taylor Caldwell, "The Middle Class Must Not Fail or All Will Be Lost," *Critique Spring/Summer*, 1983, p. 273.

178 Ibid., pp. 270-275.

179 Allen, *None Dare Call It Conspiracy*, pp. 41, 50-56. Also, Congressman Louis T. McFadden, "On The Federal Reserve Corporation," remarks in Congress, 1934, (Boston: Forum Publication Co.), p. 89.

180 Sutton, *Western Technology and Soviet Economic Development*, Vol. 3, p. 67.

181 Friedrich and Brzezinski, *Totalitarian Dictatorship and Autocracy*, p. 129.

182 Compaine, *Who Owns the Media?*

183 Ellul, *Propaganda*, pp. 102-103.

184 "Changing Times—Greater Number of Unwed Couples Living Together," UPI, *Winston-Salem Journal*, July 19, 1984, p. 6.

185 "Divorces—Nearly Triple in 20 Years," *U.S. News & World Report*, June 22, 1981, p. 12.

186 "For the First Time, White Men Are a Minority in the Work Force", Associated Press, *The Sentinel*, July 31, 1984, p. 4.

187 David Goodman, "Countdown to 1984: Big Brother May Be Right on Schedule," *The Futurist*, December 1978, p. 348.

188 Robin Wood, "Beauty Bests the Beast," *American Film*, September 1983, pp. 63-65.

189 Peter Marin, "A Revolution's Broken Promises," *Psychology Today*, July 1983, pp. 50-57.

190 Goodman, *Countdown to 1984*, p. 352.

191 Eugene H. Methvin, "TV Violence: The Shocking New Evidence," *Reader's Digest*, January 1983, p. 50.

192 Winn, *The Manipulated Mind*, pp. 72-73. Also, Peter Watson, *War on the Mind: The Military Uses and Abuses of Psychology*, (London: Hutchinson & Co., 1978), pp. 248-250.

193 Cross, *Media-Speak*, pp. 108-11.

194 "TV Program's Advisor Quits, Says Shows Demeaning to Policemen," UPI, *Winston-Salem Journal*, August 1, 1984, p. 21.

195 Cross, *Media-Speak*, p. 111.

196 Ibid., pp. 110-111. "Powers of Police Are Expanded In Court's Ruling," Associated Press, *Winston-Salem Journal*, July 6, 1984. p. 1. Richard Carelli, "Court's 'Law and Order' Tilt Popular With Conservatives," Associated Press, *Winston-Salem Journal*, July 8, 1984, p. A5.

197 Morton Mintz and Jerry S. Cohen, *Power, Inc.*, (New York: The Viking Press, 1976), pp. 3-5.

198 Ronald M. McRae, *Mind Wars: The True Story of Government Research into the Military Potential of Psychic Weapons*, New York: St. Martin's Press, 1984), p. xxvii.

199 Mintz and Cohen, *Power, Inc.*, p. 5 citing Alexander Hamilton, James Madison, and John Jay, *The Federalist*, (New York: Mentor, 1961), no. 47, p. 301.

200 Mintz and Cohen *Power, Inc.* pp. 5 & 10.

201 Allen, *None Dare Call It Conspiracy*, p. 34.

202 Weekly Compilation of Presidential Documents, February 7, 1983, Vol. 19, Number 5, p. 156.

203 "Politicizing The Word," *Time*, October 1, 1979, p. 62.

204 Kenneth Woodward and David Gates, "How The Bible Made America," *Newsweek*, December 27, 1982, pp. 44-51.

205 "Politicizing The Word" , p. 62.

206 Flo Conway and Jim Siegelman, *Holy Terror: The Fundamentalist War on America's Freedoms in Religion, Politics and Our Private Lives*, (Garden City, New York: Doubleday & Company, Inc., 1982), p. 12.

207 Mark 16:15.

208 Michael Doan, "The 'Electric Church' Spreads the Word," *U.S. News & World Report*, April 23, 1984, p. 68.

209 Conway and Siegelman, *Holy Terror*, p. 54.

210 210 Ibid., p. 231.

211 Ibid., pp. 30-31.

212 Ibid., p. 232.

213 Ibid., p. 209.

214 Gary North, *None Dare Call It Witchcraft*, (New Rochelle, New York: Arlington House Publishers, 1976), pp. 31-32. The Most comprehensive prohibition appears in Deuteronomy 18:10—12. Also, Sheila Broderick, What about... The occult, (St. Louis, Missouri: Open Door Press) for citations from both the Old and New Testament. Booklet available from the Billy Graham Evangelistic Association.

215 Richard Cavendish, ed., *Encyclopedia of the Unexplained: Magic, Occultism and Parapsychology*, (New York: McGraw-Hill Book Company, 1974), p. 153.

216 Norman McKenzie, ed., *Secret Societies*, (London: Aldous Books, 1967), p. 134.

217 Ibid., p. 137.

218 Cavendish, *Encyclopedia of the Unexplained*, p. 155.

219 Joseph Head and S. L. Cranston, ed., *Reincarnation: The Phoenix Mystery*, (New York: Julian Press/Crown Publishers, 1977), p. 134.

220 Louis Stewart, *Life Forces*, (Andrews & McNeel, Inc., 1980), p. 414.

221 Head and Cranston, *Reincarnation: The Phoenix Mystery*, p. 134.

222 Geddes MacGregor, *The Bible in the Making*, (New York: J. B. Lippincott Co., 1959)

223 Stewart, *Life Forces*, p. 280.

224 Frederic W. H. Myers, *Human Personality and its Survival of Bodily Death*, edited by Susy Smith, (New Hyde Park, New York: University Books, 1961), pp. 9-17.

225 Austin C. Lescarboura, "Edison's Views on Life and Death: An Interview with the Famous Inventor Regarding His Attempt to Communicate with the Next World," *Scientific American*, October 30, 1920, p. 446.

226 Steve Coz, "U.S. & German Researchers Reveal: We Can Talk to the Dead," *National Enquirer*, July 13, 1982, p. 55.

227 McRae, *Mind Wars*, p. 133.

228 Martin Ebon, *Psychic Warfare: Threat or Illusion?* (New York: McGraw-Hill Book Company, 1983) p. 12.

229 McRae, *Mind Wars*, p. 103.

230 Ibid., p. 29.

231 Ibid., pp. 47-48.

232 John Marks, *The Search For The Manchurian Candidate: The CIA and Mind Control*, (New York: Time Books, 1979).

233 Daniel Cohen, *Dreams, Visions & Drugs: A Search for Other Realities*, (New York: Franklin Watts, 1976). p. 41.

234 Roger A. Roffman, *Marijuana as Medicine*, (Seattle: Madrona Publishers, 1982), p. 34.

235 Cohen, *Dreams, Visions & Drugs*, pp. 42-43.

236 Brian Inglis, *The Forbidden Game* (New York: Charles Scribner's Sons, 1975), p. 12.

237 Ibid., p. 16.

238 Ibid., p. 22.

239 Roffman, *Marijuana as Medicine*, p. 76.

240 Richard Le Strange, *A History of Herbal Plants*, (New York: ARCO Publishing Co., 1977), p. 64. Also, Roffman, *Marijuana as Medicine*, p. 29 and Grinspoon, *Marihuana Reconsidered*, p. 1.

241 Roffman, *Marijuana as Medicine*, pp. 29-30.

242 Ibid., pp. 94-128. Also, Grinspoon, *Marihuana Re-considered*, pp. 218-230.

243 Grinspoon, *Marihuana Reconsidered*, p. 29.

244 Ibid., p. 327.

245 Ibid., p. 226.

246 Roffman, *Marijuana as Medicine*, p. 26.

247 Grinspoon, *Marihuana Reconsidered*, p. 251.

248 Inglis, *The Forbidden Game*, p. 165.

249 *The Occult Technology of Power*, p. 45.

250 Ibid., p. 10.

251 Grinspoon, *Marihuana Reconsidered*, p. 173.

252 Inglis, *The Forbidden Game*, p. 32.

253 Grinspoon, *Marihuana Reconsidered*, p. 156.

254 Winn, *The Manipulated Mind*, p. 36.

255 Ibid., pp. 36-53.

256 Francis Hitching, "Where Darwin Went Wrong," *Reader's Digest*, September 1982, pp. 9-16. Francis Hitching, "Was Darwin Wrong?" *Life*, Vol. 5, April 1982, pp. 48-52.

257 Bjorn Kurten, *Not From The Apes*, (New York: Pantheon Books, 1972), p. 121.

258 William Dudley Pelley, *Soulcraft*, (Noblesville, Indiana: Fellowship Press, Inc., 1950), Vol. 1, Chapter 2, p. 6.

259 Pelley, *Soulcraft*, Vol. 2, Chapter 26, pp. 3-22.

260 William Dudley Pelley, *Adam Awakes*, (Noblesville, Indiana: Fellowship Press, 1953), pp. 52-61; Pelley, *Soulcraft*, Vol. 1, Chapter 2, pp. 9-18; Vol. 6, Chapter 75, pp. 11-12.

261 *The Golden Scripts* (Noblesville, Indiana: Fellowship Press, 1941), Chapter 165, pp. 578-579.

262 Pelley, *Soulcraft*, Vol. 1, Chapter 2, pp. 9-18.

263 McRae, *Mind Wars*, p. 53.

264 Pelley, *Soulcraft*, Vol. 2, Chapter 18, p. 16.

265 Dr. Joseph Murphy, *The Power of Your Subconscious Mind*, (Englewood Cliffs: Prenctice-Hall, 1963), p. 28.

266 Ibid., p. 34.

267 Matthew 21:22.

268 Dina Ingber, "Brain Breathing," *Science Digest*, June 1981, pp. 72+.

269 Philip S. Foner, ed., *The Complete Writings of Thomas Paine*, (New York: The Citadel Press, 1945), "The American Crisis No. 1," p. 50.

270 *The Golden Scripts*, pp. 583-588.

271 Pamela Weintraub, "Evolution's Child," *Omni*, August 193, p. 102.

272 Sharon Begley with John Carey, "Man's Family Portrait," *Newsweek*, April 23, 1984, p. 50.

273 Hitching, *Where Darwin Went Wrong*, p. 14.

274 Stanley N. Wellborn, "Life Beyond Earth: The Search Intensifies," *U.S. News & World Report*, September 10, 1984.

275 Henry C. Clausen, *Your Amazing Mystic Powers*, (Washington, DC: Supreme Council, Mother Council of the World, of the Inspectors General Knights Commander of the House of the Temple of Solomon of the 33rd Degree of the Ancient and Accepted Scottish Rite of Freemasonry of the Southern Jurisdiction of the United States of America, 1985), p.35.